North Country

North Country

A Pedagogical Almanac

Carolyn J. Dekker

www.blacklawrence.com

Executive Editor: Diane Goettel
Cover Design: Matthew Revert
Cover Art: "Quincy Mine" by Adam Johnson
Book Design: Amy Freels

ISBN: 978-1-62557-052-9

Published 2022 by Black Lawrence Press.
Printed in the United States.

Contents

2015

August
Migration

We are strange creatures, my dog and I, migrating north as the summer wanes. In the five years I spent in Ann Arbor before moving back to New England, I never entered Michigan's Upper Peninsula, its true north. Now, Beckett and I strike out from New England on familiar highways, pass a few days with friends in Ann Arbor, and then turn north. I've never measured the five hundred miles from Ann Arbor to Hancock in hands on the wheel and feet on the pedals. This is the kind of long-haul driving that can take you from Washington, DC, to Maine, or indeed, DC to Detroit. Michigan is this large.

When we near the Mackinac Bridge, the only point of contact between Michigan's upper and lower peninsulas, I exit the highway to walk around near the old lighthouse and the colonial trading post that once dispatched shipments of beaver pelts and *Panis*—enslaved Native Americans—to the markets of New France. The day is cloudy and the wind blows spray off Lake Huron, pressing Beckett's long black hair flat against his body. There is no one to take my picture, so I take his with the bridge in the background. I'm aiming for *Bold Border Collie, About to Emigrate*, but the wind makes him look like he's cringing, his white-tipped tail blown in a question mark around his haunches.

I look at the bridge, five miles of elegant cable suspension, and I open the door to feeling. I'm nervous; I'm excited; I'm profoundly, vertiginously alone. My husband of ten years has decided not to follow me. But here I am, headed north anyway: out of one life and into another.

Beckett and I cross over the Straits of Mackinac and enter the upper country. The change after the bridge is immediate. Instead of exits, there are roadside businesses selling venison jerky, Wisconsin cheese curds, and pasties—the small hand pies that Cornish miners brought to the region. Then we leave even these outposts behind. We forge west along the sandy north shore of Lake Michigan, hang a right at some deserted vacation cabins, and strike north across the peninsula's narrow waist. The Upper Peninsula is more than three hundred miles from east to west at its widest point, but in places, only thirty or forty miles of land separate its southern and northern shores.

Driving through eighty miles of almost uninterrupted national forest, I have a chance to appreciate the scale of the pine forests and the small scope of the human presence in them. In Marquette, the Upper Peninsula's largest city at thirty thousand people, I pull in for a moment at the faded strip mall that houses Marquette Soo Bahk Do. It's the middle of the day and the martial arts studio is closed, but I catch my breath and let myself look forward to the training I will do here, having already exchanged cheery e-mails with the instructor. I paw at my supply of snacks, which is nearly exhausted, and offer the dog a pretzel.

Up the road, I leave Beckett in the car long enough to buy a cup of gas station coffee, and the long, hypnotizing miles of pine forest outside of Marquette soon make me glad I did. The sleek, modern campus of Michigan Technological University pounces out of the trees when I finally reach Houghton. The buildings, the largest I've seen for a hundred miles, are a strange apparition.

I rumble onto the brick main street of downtown Houghton and, surrounded by nineteenth-century storefronts, find myself translocated in history once more. I stop the car and take Beckett out for another photograph with a bridge behind him. The squat, massive lift bridge spans the Portage Canal that separates Houghton and Hancock. It's the only way on or off the northern part of the Keweenaw Peninsula that will be our home. Both Hancock and Houghton slope down sharply toward the waterway, giving the towns a stacked appearance that draws my eye across the water and upward past buildings and roof peaks and toward the forested hill top, crowned by the shaft house of the Quincy Mine.

Views that draw the eye upward have a way of lifting the heart, too. This steep terrain told me at first glance that I could love this place. I lift a prayer for happiness and home. I look at Beckett scenting the air and think with wonder that this may be the last new homecoming for this dog who's come with me from Ann Arbor to Massachusetts to Maine and back during my itinerant, career-fledging years.

After a brief stop at the realtor's office, I drive to our new home and take the last photo of the day. Beckett, with a look of wild glee in his eye, stands near the open front door. I leave the housekey dangling in the lock, drop the leash, and let him charge inside.

2015

September
Beginning

The very first thing I ask my first-year students to do is write about themselves, where they come from, and what they dream of. I do the exercise myself by way of introduction and model. The dreams I name—applying my talents to serve my students and finding a little community here—feel like enough to hope for. I know so little of the riches this place will hold for me.

My students share their dreams with me. One young man works summers fishing in Alaska and is saving money to buy a little piece of land in the Copper Country and start a family with his girlfriend. Another wants to follow his mother into nursing. A young woman who has overcome a sports injury wants to become a physical therapist. A biology major has med school dreams, and a historian sets her sights on law school. They are either proudly local or are athletes recruited from farther afield.

My students' skill levels range widely. Some are serviceable writers. Others seem wholly unacquainted with punctuation or complete sentences. The most elegant writer in the class is a young man from Detroit named Dan. He writes passionately about wanting to use his education to show his younger siblings back home a pathway to success. Enamored of his graceful sentences and his love of reading, I dream of recruiting him as an English major.

He tells me that he wants to be a point guard in the NBA. I'll see this again and again over the years: male students, often smaller than me, who hope to play professional basketball or baseball or football. I'm always dismayed and confused when students seem unaware of the differences between Division I and Division III athletics. The role of intercollegiate athletics at a small college like ours is essentially recreational. As a former and far-from-gifted college athlete myself, I don't find their passion for sports misplaced, but I do find the expectation of a payoff concerning. Division III colleges offer no athletic scholarships, and professional teams do not scout here. Some of our alumni have played stints in professional basketball in Europe, enjoying the travel and the chance to live abroad, but it's not the NBA and it's not a living.

Dan doesn't last a month in college. He stops coming to class, and when I try to send the basketball coach after him, I learn that he hasn't even joined the team. Finally, Dan tells me that his family wants him back home, but he's waiting until they can send money for a bus ticket. Alarmed that time is ticking down for him to get a refund for his tuition and room and board, I find him a ride.

He keeps in touch with me down the years, including the night he calls me from jail, having been pulled over while attempting to visit Hancock. It's midnight and he's five hours from me in the great piney nothing south of the Mackinaw Bridge. I can't miss my morning class to get him, but I go out to fill the gas tank of the friend he finds to make the retrieval. As I phone the jail to update him, I use the Doctor in front of my name, and when they ask me who I am, I say that I'm his professor, articulating sharply, as if I can push my white privilege through the phoneline and throw it over him like a cloak.

I imagined when I started working here that I would invest in students for four years and then wave them off into their futures. I didn't understand what a forty-four percent graduation rate feels like. It means saying goodbye after two years, or a term, or just a few weeks. It means writing letters in support of transfer applications. It means watching students have their college hopes upended by events in their and their families' lives that more affluent students might have been able to weather. It means students who melt out of the classroom without a goodbye.

My university is not uniquely dysfunctional. Two-thirds of our students are eligible for federal Pell Grants, meaning that most of our students have family incomes of less than fifty thousand dollars per year. At my former employer, Bates College, just eleven percent of students are Pell-eligible. I used to walk past the old Victorian that housed the Bates admissions office on my way home from teaching and see the admissions team sitting around a large conference table, looking up applicants' family home values on Zillow. They were playing hunches to find families who might be wealthy enough to pay the entire sixty-eight thousand dollars-per-year price tag. My alma mater, Williams, is so well-endowed that it is one of the rare institutions that can afford to practice need-blind admissions instead of thumbing the scales in favor of wealthy kids, so twenty percent of its students are Pell-eligible.

College is the single most effective tool that America currently employs to foster upward social mobility. The Pell numbers make a handy index for the proportion of a student body who is seeking an education that could utterly transform their socioeconomic reality. But nationwide, the six-year graduation rate for Pell recipients hovers under fifty percent. Poor students struggle to finish college in America.

Low-income students who manage to claw their way into elite colleges gain access to the formidable academic and financial resources of those institutions, where per-student spending often far exceeds even their shocking sticker prices. These students frequently persist and make use of this ladder to opportunity. Students who land at working-class institutions like mine are also handed a chance, but it's a high-stakes gamble that can have ghastly consequences.

The students who exit American colleges and universities without degrees but with student loan debt spend their lifetimes poorer than students who seek no further education after high school. The non-graduates are maimed for life and would have been far, far better off if a recruiter had never come calling. My university produces joyful graduates in blue robes each May and successful alumni who are proud of all they've overcome, but it also produces this long-lasting harm. America has decided that it's not enough for students to invest four years of life and effort in their college education; they must mortgage their futures on it, too.

I don't tell this to my students on the first day of school. Instead, I ask them to center their dreams in our classroom and enlist me in their cheering section. I'll stay in that section for life. Five years on, Dan drops me a note. He has two little boys named for prophets and he tells me my babies will be erudite. I think his will be, too.

2015

October
Pomegranates

Thursday, the first of October. My parents arrive tomorrow. I should be home, cleaning the house of dog hair and empty coffee mugs and drifts of clean laundry, removing the signs of my bachelor disorganization. Instead, I am searching Hancock for pomegranates. As with most food products whose scarcity provokes my self-mocking frustration (quinoa, fresh basil, vegetarian bullion), I finally find them at the food co-op.

Tomorrow my first-year writing classes are discussing Andrea Scarpino's "Self-Portrait as Pomegranate" and "Madonna of the Pomegranate." The Upper Peninsula's poet laureate has chosen as one of her favorite motifs a fruit that is nearly impossible to obtain in this northern clime, so far from money and markets.

I take the pomegranates to the counter. They are organic and somewhat paltry. They cost a dollar seventy-nine each. I hope four will be enough. I think of other things I have bought for my classroom and know I cannot spend seven dollars on every lesson. But at some checkouts, a dollar seventy-nine might buy a king-sized candy bar. What tawdry royalty—when here it buys "Eve's temptation, / Adam's lust," Persephone's journey to the underworld.

"She be headed down there soon," says one of my students, laughing, after we've pooled our knowledge of the myth. I love and encourage this kind of alert rowdiness in my classroom.

He's right about Persephone. The days are still hot, but the mornings have the bite of coming frost. If I'm going to get my garage roof replaced before the snow closes in, this is the weekend. This is why my father is coming to visit.

I ask a student to read the first poem. While she does so, I unsheathe my hunting knife, withdraw a plate from my bag, hold a pomegranate above the plate, and cut. First I make a delicate ring, then with one plunge and a twist of the wrist, I open the fruit with hardly any spatter. I wish someone would look up to see me flourishing the luminous seeds, but my students' eyes track Scarpino's words across the page. When they finally look up, I have the fruit in eighths on the plate and someone asks, "What is that?"

It's a question I anticipated. It's why the pomegranate is here.

"You've never seen a pomegranate before?" another student asks.

"No!"

"It's okay," I say. "Me neither, until I got to college."

I do not often stand upon blue-collar pedigree, but, determined to normalize this unfamiliarity with exotic commodities, I turn to the board and mutter comically, "Construction worker's kid, what do I know about a pomegranate?"

"See? Yeah!" says the first student.

This is close to the red heart of the thing. When I arrived at college fourteen years ago, a pomegranate was as mythical to me as a unicorn.

The first pomegranate I saw was in the small, fine hands of my friend Masha, someone I couldn't have imagined before she appeared in my life, living across the hall from me in my freshman dorm. A Russian émigré from a Boston suburb, her parents used to visit and bring her elaborate deliveries of food from home, things you wouldn't find in a tiny western Massachusetts town: soft powdery cookies and pies—long homemade flat bread filled with cabbage. There were Russian grocery items, too: malted drinks; sweet halva made from sunflower seeds; black, thin-sliced rye bread; and, yes, pomegranates. Masha's mother was an educator and a theatre director, and she spoke easily of Vladimir Nabokov and David Foster Wallace. Her father was a software designer; her grandmother, a physicist. I had never dreamt of such progenitors.

Masha's mother had told her that the fruit of a pomegranate is red and iron-rich, something a young woman ought to eat while menstruating. As Masha extended a sliver of that fruit to me, a sliver of that caring, I knew I was glimpsing a kind of mothering, a frank loving of a daughter or a friend in her whole body, a category of love whose existence in the world I hadn't guessed at.

Masha and I might have been lovers, if I could have found a sexual vocabulary for my fascination with where she came from; my admiration for her taste in literature, fashion, and punk music; my delight in her creativity and her sharp, sarcastic wit; and the heart-thrilling way her small shoulders fit under my arm. I grew up too slowly. Did I miss something that would have bound us closer?

On the roof, my father works with casual power: twice as smooth, twice as fast as me. When we begin to tear off the old roof, he strips half of the first side by himself while I putter back and forth, throwing shingles on the tarp, bagging the brown paper flour sacks that some homeowner half a century ago thriftily substituted for tarpaper.

Sixty-two and with one hip replaced, he walks with a limp—not so much from the surgery as from too many years spent bracing himself against pain. This is my roof, and I have been an intensely physical person all my life, but here he is, protecting me from the real and brutal work of it.

Finally, I take the pitchfork. He counsels aggression, says to push the tines hard into the rows of shingles from the side and lift fast to pop the nails. There are three layers of shingles, and thrice the nails make for hard stabbing and hard lifting. He roves the planks he's cleared with a hammer and small pry bar, removing nails with two-handed grace. Later, taking up the same job, I pull what I can one-handed and hammer the pry bar under the stubborn nails. One, two, three, five taps. Without looking up, I can hear him working and know he gets each nail with only three. It's not his strength, really, that tells on this work, but the confident, coordinated knowledge in his hands.

After lunch, we work down from the ridgeline onto the south side of the roof. I find I prefer the flat shovel to his pitchfork, so we both attack the same task, gouging away at the layered asphalt from above. For a little while, I am almost keeping pace. Then somehow he is beside me, helping on my side again.

That night, I tell a friend how thoroughly I have been outworked. Trying to comfort me, my friend compares my father's build to that of a Kodiak bear. But my father was once as young and willowy as I. That was long ago, before his years at a desk but after his first decade and a half of physical labor, those years that left a legacy of cracked vertebrae, bulging discs, and a quiet, confident knowledge of how to rebuild or repair every part of a home that can weather, rot, or wear out. I think of a childhood photograph of him holding me on his hip. In it he is wearing the soft light gray sweater I reach for on chilly mornings twenty-five years later.

If my father works me under the table, it is not because he has the build of a Kodiak bear. It's because he still has the heart of that willowy young man who swung his daughter aloft, who carried boards, hung drywall, took the debris of old Philadelphia apartments and a wrecked house in Dover and made them all bright and new.

I want to tell my father about my new life here, what it means to me to live on the northern edge of beyond; to teach these students of Detroit, Calumet, and Escanaba; to tell him why I will stay, husband or no (and it will be no). Perhaps at some level my parents know this already, hence this journey to help me handle the roof and to check on their only daughter, alone and with winter bearing down on her in this new place.

In my imagination of this project, my father and I have long talks on the roof. In reality, the closest we come is the two hundred mile journey to buy shingles, tarpaper, flashing, and trim. We depart before dawn on Sunday, and the rising sun reveals pillars of fog marching across Keweenaw Bay and then touches flame orange in the trees. The banks of cloud stand over Marquette like a mountain range.

On the way home, I tell myself. On the way home, we can talk.

Two hours later, I'm huddled in my coat, highway noise in my ear, ten feet of aluminum flashing speared through the car and poking out the window above my shoulder. It's too loud to speak. I turn up the volume on the car stereo and then doze off with my chin on the pile of lumber, the scent of fresh pine in my nostrils.

Wednesday is the longest day. I rush home from the classroom and find my father already on the roof, slowly nailing down the fourth row of shingles.

My father loves craftsmanship in all its forms. I have seen him wax rhapsodic over a well-tied fly, a woodturned urn of mesquite and bloodwood on a museum pedestal, a perfect darkroom exposure, and the best bulldozer driver he ever saw. His love of doing a task right has led him to cut a small piece of trim as a spacer and to use scrap plywood to build a frame to guide me as I cut the shorter shingles that begin each row.

I change back into my tarry work clothes and tear open more bundles of shingles. After a moment's hesitation about how best to use me, he lets me take the spacing block from him.

His facility with the nail gun, even on uneven planking, keeps me working at full tilt, sliding each shingle in front of him. I hold it steady until the second nail goes in and then I reach for the next. Occasionally, after I scurry for more shingles or another coil of nails, I nudge a shingle with the spacer and answer "Yep" to the unasked question of "Ready?"

When we fall into wordless, efficient rhythm, the neat rows of shingles grow steadily under us. I feel happy and proud.

We work until dark, and then, knowing it will rain tomorrow, we get headlamps and work beyond it. I haul the last bundles of shingles onto the roof to spare him trips up and down the ladder. We do not talk. But maybe the work is the heart of it.

In the last of my classes on that Friday before my parents arrived, I reached for the final pomegranate, but as I cut it, it fell open too easily. Instead of an intricate ruby treasure, I found brown paste inside. Quickly, I hid it back inside my bag, wiped the knife blade, and divided and divided again until I made one pomegranate do for fourteen students.

As I walked the rows, handing out the fruit, my heart was on the plate alongside it. But then, my heart is always trembling outstretched in this room, saying to my students, This is what college should be. This is what I want for you. Eat the mythical foods, discuss poetry and Greek mythology and Italian renaissance paintings, the whole world yours and all its jeweled fruits.

2017

October
Apples and Time Machines

I am always most in love with the season that is just passing out of reach. On the first of October, I run shirtless through the forest and plunge over the dunes into Lake Superior with my dog. Summer! Summer in October! my heart sings.

I cannot quite admit I'm having my last swim of the season even though this morning, when I rose early to do trail work, there was a whisper of frost edging the leaves of our juneberry tree. Using a weed-whacker to clear undergrowth out in the woods, I came upon a false Solomon's seal in fruit. It was so red that at first I took it for a discarded toy. All these signs, yet I craved another beach afternoon, another armload of tomatoes from the garden. Summer had me in its thrall: the golden light, the long, bright northern evenings, the cold plunge into blue-watered lakes. For one afternoon in October, summer gave me that last embrace, though the fall semester was already five weeks underway.

For two weeks, my students and I have been reading Octavia Butler's *Kindred.* I have a love-hate relationship with time-travel narratives. They teach beautifully, but I have reservations about them as art. The jolly schmuck who gets to meet Billy Shakespeare or King Arthur makes me squeamish; the encounters feel too unserious to be useful tools with which to confront the weight of history.

Maybe I read Kurt Vonnegut too late in life. I missed him in high school when his literary-bad-boy aura might have most appealed. I finally read *Slaughterhouse-Five* in graduate school while filling in classics and hunting texts for a course in war literature. I admired the way Vonnegut called out atrocity on all sides, as in: "I have lit my way in a prison at night with candles from the fat of human beings who were butchered by the brothers and fathers of those schoolgirls who were boiled... alive in a water tower by my own countrymen." Yet I found myself roving the hallways of the university, groaning aloud at the idea of teaching *Slaughterhouse-Five*. The lines above are testimony that the main character Billy Pilgrim delivers to an assembly of Tralfamadorians—time-traveling, one-eyed space aliens who are shaped like toilet plungers. The framing of the Holocaust and Dresden with such absurdity made me cringe.

One of my mentors, himself born in England to a Jewish refugee family, heard out my reservations and simply looked at me and said, "Well, Carolyn, he was there."

Yes, indeed. Kurt Vonnegut huddled with his fellow prisoners of war in a meat locker while allied bombing destroyed the historic wooden city of Dresden. He and his comrades walked out of the slaughterhouse the next morning to confront a moonscape of leveled buildings and the carbonized bodies of civilians who had tried to take refuge in cellars. If Vonnegut determined that the telling of this story requires Tralfamadorians, who was I to quibble? I taught the book.

Likewise, I teach *Kindred* with one eye on the entry-points into history it provides for my students and the other on my own discomfort. On this semester's re-reading, I am struck by the way Butler constantly acknowledges the insufficiency of even time travel to allow Dana, a self-confident Black woman from 1976, to know a slave's experience. Dana feels guilty for the ease with which she and her husband fit into antebellum Maryland because she knows they "weren't really in." She elaborates: "We were observers watching a show. We were watching history happen around us. And we were actors. While we waited to go home, we humored the people around us by pretending to be like them." Lodged within her own disruptive, impossible presence in the 1810s and 20s is an irresistible and buoying teleology: the birth of her ancestress is coming; emancipation is coming in 1862; after it, 1976 is coming. Dana is physically beaten, humiliated, and even threatened with rape, but there is no sequence of events that will ever allow her to fully approach the experience of slavery as undergone by someone for whom it had no promised end date. For Butler, time travel's disruption of verisimilitude is a constant reminder that in art, there is never an equals sign.

By asking if Butler or Vonnegut ought to be using time travel in this way, by extension, I'm asking questions that otherwise do not occur to me—should Toni Morrison or Edward P. Jones or Colson Whitehead or anyone muck around in the traumas of slavery and tell stories about them? Should Leslie Marmon Silko, Tim O'Brien, and Phil Klay write war stories? Fiction writers weave stories that are vital for continuing to contest and correct the American historical imaginary. Historiography shapes what we know as fact; fiction, and the best of creative nonfiction, shapes what we know with our hearts. I am by no means of the belief that serious literary fiction must confine itself to realism: Morrison, Jones, and Whitehead all deploy speculative fiction elements to great effect, and few writers are more formally inventive than Morrison, Silko, or O'Brien. In my aversion to time travel, I'm not just recoiling from genre but also from Butler's overt nudging at her readers to see the futility and artificiality of the transport that fiction offers us.

During one of Dana's early experiences in the 1800s, Butler explicitly compares time travel (and books) to other ways of understanding slavery. Perhaps Butler is thinking of *Roots*, aired just two years before *Kindred* was published, when Dana thinks:

> I had seen people beaten on television and in the movies. I had seen the too-red blood substitute streaked across their backs and heard their well-rehearsed screams. But I hadn't lain nearby and smelled their sweat or heard them pleading and praying, shamed before their families and themselves.

Though Dana ultimately concludes that even the supernatural experience of time travel does not make her "really in," in this early passage Butler makes a claim for the power of fiction, and this time-travel book in particular, to connect readers to a deeper understanding of history. Fiction, she claims, can use sensory description to engage *more* senses than film or television and can enable the leap of empathy that Dana quickly demonstrates when she bears witness to the man's shame as well as his pain. For Dana, this kind of closeness to the pain and danger of slavery is a horrifying realization. For Butler, however, it's also a kind of boast, one she continues to make good on more than forty years later as *Kindred* enjoys a wide readership and a place in high school and college pedagogies. Butler correctly pegged American readers as having an enduring need to use fiction to approach the history of slavery.

What does it say about the American psyche that we need these fictional narratives to suture us to our own national history? We need stories—new ones every year—as bulwarks thrown up against a national tendency to forget and minimize. I can't help finding something disappointing in our need to be inserted as eyewitness. I want historiography and first-hand slave narratives to be enough, without this need for the time-travel tourist visa and its mania for inserting the modern witness into the past. If time travel is a metaphor for the activities of books and readers, perhaps my squeamishness with time travel is my discomfort with the project of fiction itself.

I make an exception for one time-travel narrative. I believe in Audrey Niffenegger's *The Time Traveler's Wife* entirely. It is the perfect time-travel narrative, being perfectly honest about the fundamental solipsism of the device. In the nature of Henry's travel, his visitation of his wife Claire's childhood, I see my own ravenous desires to know every piece of my own lover's life. The fierce, mutually self-interested entanglement of lovers who want to know each other's stories is the perfect scale on which to play out a time-travel narrative. Such stories are always about the traveler's fierce and impossible need to see the past *for themselves*. At times, we are all that time-traveler. Finding myself in new love, I can relate.

Shawn and I began at the deep end, moving in together after less than a year's courtship and a handful of visits because of our sense that the only viable time to relocate our younger daughter was at the beginning of her ninth grade year. Now, a year into our life as a blended family, we're all still learning each other.

One night, Shawn and I settle down for a few hours' rest together before a night shift will take him from our bed at midnight. We watch the film of *The Time Traveler's Wife*. It's rare I can sit still long enough to watch a movie, but *Kindred* has put time-travel narratives on my mind, so *The Time Traveler's Wife* feels a little like research.

I feel the storm of my emotions building as the film wends to its conclusion, but am still surprised when the fierce rush of tears breaks over me like a wave. Niffenegger's story is as ravenous as my heart. I sobbed hard for the thirty-eight years of my beloved's life I wasn't around to share, for the young childhood of our daughters.

I am by nature greedy, hungry, and competitive. I am often amazed that Shawn wants to live next to all of my outsized feeling, my hunger and striving. My usual response to these feelings in myself is suppression and no small measure of shame. I want the impossible but rarely let myself cry over it. For this one moment, I mourn the lost years. He stays with me in the storm of all this wanting and holds me with bemused tenderness, missing his nap before the midnight shift.

Our youngest, Mackenna, was only thirteen when I first met her, gawky and storklike and on her way to being beautiful and graceful. Our eldest, Heliena, was sixteen and already uncannily adult, a small, wide-cheekboned version of Shawn. Shawn and I talked for the first time at a martial arts tournament banquet somewhere in Indiana. The girls flitted between our table and the pack of kids on the dance floor and already I felt Shawn's past and the girls' childhoods tugging at my heart. His stories of their toddler antics gave me a sense that I'd missed out on those years. Who was I to feel such a thing? I hugged him goodnight when the bar closed, still trying to understand the longing I felt and why this parting from a new acquaintance felt like a momentous goodbye.

When we found ourselves sitting together at breakfast, Shawn, the girls, and I, it had a courtly, awkward morning-after glow, as if we hadn't parted ways on the hotel stairs just a few hours before. As I drove away, I was still asking myself where I'd been all those years. I felt an abyss opening under everything I knew of my life. This was the feeling of the rest of my life beckoning me into it. Having never been called so before, I didn't know that the whisper of the future would feel like the tug of the past.

Instead of following the wild impulse to aim my car straight for Detroit, I let my life take me to Maine, then to Massachusetts. I did not see my family again until another tournament in another city sixteen months later. More lost time.

My husband assembles himself from the ground up every morning. Sitting up, placing his feet firm and flat on the bedroom floor, knees wide, he leans forward over his feet and stands. Men with back injuries do not roll or spring out of bed. They build themselves. They put their boxers on deliberately, sometimes while gripping the furniture. They are wary of sneezing too early in the morning.

We share versions of this history—one moment I am fighting, flinging after my sparring partner, leaving the ground, left middle roundhouse, right high. My partner's smile acknowledges the headshot, then fades from his face as I land badly, my knee twisting, a high-pitched shriek leaving my lips. One moment I'm kicking a dazzlingly talented master in the head; the next I'm lying on my back, my lower leg numb, wondering what happened. The question won't be answered for two months, rural medicine being what it is. An ACL tear.

His version: one moment he is jumping, simultaneously lifting both knees and delivering punishing blows to two targets at face height. *Ssang baal ahp cha na gi.* Split kick. Eagle kick. Power and beauty. The next he is landing badly, half a lifetime of industrial work catching up with him in one moment. A compressed disc in his spine, and he can hardly crawl to his bedroom door the next morning.

I wasn't there to take him to the doctor or ease the burdens of single-parenting while in pain. I also wasn't around to see him when he could still fly. I can only gather a picture of it from what I still see on the good days—his explosive power off the ground, beautiful spinning hook kicks, the trailing leg tucked high. Even today, he's a better jumper than I have ever dreamed of being.

What am I to do with this wistfulness I feel for a past I never saw? When we square off now, we are a good match, his power balanced by my extra four inches of reach. He can't jump as much as he'd like. I can't do everything I'd like with my dominant leg, because I can't always trust my left leg to stand or land on. But on a good day, if the two of us throw off our pads and have a match, bareknuckled and swift, at the end of sparring class, the young martial artists I teach stop and stare in open admiration. I want this now to be enough.

The girls go away for the weekend in mid-October. Their absence leaves our little house echoing. We make the effort to craft the perfect fall weekend for ourselves. On Friday we chase the northern lights out to the cliff's edge at the state park where we held our wedding celebration in high summer. Bundled against the cold, I fuss with the camera, opening it to the wide green arc on the horizon. We drive home under a dazzle of stars and lay down beside the wood stove.

For this night and every other, we share a twin mattress. I'm a restless sleeper but I find comfort in the way Shawn's motions in sleep follow my tossings across the bed. I wake sometimes with my face pillowed on the smooth skin of his shoulder blade, or my cheek on his collar bone. I delight in these tangles, this slow motion passion of fitting together my long angles and his muscular curves. Sometimes, I twine my fingers in his hair and rest the bridges of my feet under his arches, having and holding him from top to bottom. This is the now. This is enough.

On Saturday I wake him with pancakes and we head to the barn together. I saddle Rocky, the paint horse I lease, and clip a lead rope to his hackamore. Shawn mounts up and the three of us set off together. Shawn enjoyed horses in childhood summers at Boy Scout camp before he grew up to become dreadfully allergic to horses, hay, and barns in general, and then become the father of two horsey daughters. He suffers the dust we track home from the barn and listens, half-comprehending, to our horse talk. Today, he even comes out to ride, swaying along uncertainly as I lead his horse.

Behind the farm is a piece of property with an abandoned apple orchard on it, a reminder of the Keweenaw's more populous past. Rocky hasn't been off the farm alone before—at least not since he and I became acquainted in June. When he pauses at mud puddles or bends in the trail, I let him look around and then gently coax him on. Horse and rider together make a centaur slightly less brave than the more courageous member of the pair. Walking beside me, though, Rocky feels accompanied.

The ragged post-logging regrowth on the hills around us is warming to soft brown with oak leaves and lighting up yellow and red-orange where there are small stands of aspen and maple. We brave a narrow, tunnel-like trail through some aspen and step into the orchard meadow. We go from tree to tree, Shawn standing in the stirrups to pick high and I picking low, until we fill my backpack with these apples that no one comes to tend. Rocky is patient with our pauses and windings through tall grass and blackberry brambles that have turned fire-red with fall. He stays close to my side, reaching out to nudge and nuzzle me and remind himself he is not alone. Surrounded by apples and autumn hills, I sigh happily. "I'm ready for it to be fall now," I say.

At home, we cut the apples for apple butter, feeling rich astonishment at the harvest. We've been given all this out of the land's past and nature's good care. One of the apples is a bright, pale red. I can smell how sweet it is as soon as my knife splits it. It tastes like what a Red Delicious wishes it were. Others, my favorites, are green and fiercely tart, bringing water to the mouth in an almost painful rush. Nearly all of the apples are spotted and scarred, but under the scars, the flesh is sound and white.

As the apples cook down and the house fills with the scent of cinnamon, I can already feel my heart bracing for the end of this season.

The turning of the year always seems to make me aware that life's time machine moves in just one direction. To love or to tell stories is to stretch our hearts out over the unbridgeable gulf that extends behind us and before us—be it a season or thirteen years or a hundred and sixty. Within my best love is always this ache of loss. But maybe, for this ever-moving world, that will do.

2016

November
How We Make Do

I know the Keweenaw is home when I walk into a local thrift store and see a corner shelf devoted to half-empty bottles of shampoo. I don't jump at the bargain, but I recognize the impulse that brings them to the sales floor. This town is home to people who think, Surely there must still be some use in this. Over the course of many slow browsing trips at the local thrift stores, I buy plates and mugs, flannel shirts, a dresser, countless flower pots and picture frames, sheets and towels. I buy canning jars, too, though in the years before our region finally begins to recycle glass, I have to be careful not to accidentally spend a quarter on a plain spaghetti sauce jar that won't take a Ball lid.

I love this community with its skills for making last and making do, though I learn to watch out for it, too. Open a wall or floor in any hundred-year-old building in town, and you may find creative repairs fit to make a building inspector back away in horror. I've seen cracked floor joists splinted with a little plywood, two-by-fours standing in for banisters, a shower light fixture made from a Hills Bros. coffee can. These fixes roam the roads, too: the rust-obliterated frame of a classic Bronco pieced together with lumber, drive shafts made from the square stock legs of street signs, chimeric pickup trucks that go through two or three makes from nose to tailgate. I admire the ingenuity, but I wouldn't want to drive it. Objects have a different life cycle here, caught in an eddy where they turn through many seasons until they truly live to the end of their use.

My husband's first employment in town is on the floor at JCPenney, just in time for the Thanksgiving-to-Christmas rush. The job comes with minimum wage and a requirement that he wear red shirts, a color he considers uniquely unflattering. JCPenney is willing to sell him some, of course, but we decide to try the local consignment store first. This is how I find myself standing in an icy November wind after my teaching day is done instead of walking home. I'm waiting for my husband to pick me up for red shirt shopping.

While I'm waiting, I'm chatting with a student who's suffering in the wind, too. His legs glow pink through big, flapping holes in his blue jeans. I'm nervous because there's an opportunity here.

My colleague put me up to it. He thought I would have the—what?—tact? chumminess?—to pull it off. This star pupil, a bright-as-blazes sophomore, is one of those rare students who could have succeeded at any college but has chosen this one. Some years ago, the college agreed to pay the township for some land by educating the high school's graduates on scholarship. This young man is riding that opportunity for all it's worth, living independently, working full time in a restaurant kitchen, and making straight As.

But those pants. My colleague is worried.

To be honest, I hadn't noticed them. Not so long ago, I was teaching in the Environmental Studies department at a college in Maine where the scruffiest students were often the wealthiest. Ragged clothing was more likely to signify a countercultural commitment to limit consumption or a joyous embrace of freedom from private high-school dress codes than it was to indicate financial desperation. I planned to file my colleague's concern and do nothing about it.

But then I found myself here, chatting with this exact student and waiting for a ride to the consignment store on the edge of town.

I ask my student if I can take him with us and buy him a few pairs of pants.

He flinches and straightens visibly, his pride wounded. He can afford pants, he tells me, he just doesn't care.

I feel a flash of recognition—here is one of my people—and a simultaneous horror at having been lured into playing the role of the eyes and the voice of the world's judgement. Silently cursing my colleague, I retreat like a coward behind the line, "Your professors are worried." I'm only digging the hole deeper, making this more mortifying for both of us. My partner pulls up and I flee.

Some years on, this student will evolve into a sharp dresser and appear in my classroom one morning in an excellent leather jacket. I'll compliment it and he'll proudly announce that it's a thrift-store find. We'll enthuse together over secondhand clothing, and I'll still wonder, in the back of my mind, at the conformist damage I may have done to him in my fumbling effort to get him into a whole pair of pants. Surely there were workplaces and judgements enough waiting for him. I should have allowed him a few more years of dressing to suit his own conscience and whims.

I'm learning hard lessons about taking a direct approach to student needs. I forge close relationships with students, sometimes in my classroom and sometimes as their martial arts instructor. At least once a term, I get wind that a young person I'm invested in is bookless. I can't stand to know a twenty-thousand dollar-per year education is going to be wrecked over a few hundred dollars in books. In my first year on campus, I buy math and business and sociology textbooks for students, as well as extras for my classes. I become the gadfly who chases down other instructors in parking lots to ask if students can use older editions of their assigned textbooks.

"Why are you asking?" says a business professor, baffled.

I tell him, with some rage, "Because I'm sick of seeing students fail their classes because they don't have books."

And when I get the books, the students thank me. This is in its own way unbearable. These students, disproportionately Black and Latino, are now thanking their white teacher for these small, necessary gifts when it is they who bring the Pell Grants, the student loans, the earnings of summer work and parents' strivings that make the whole university system run. Who should be thanking who?

I know with what hardship and sacrifice students find the tuition and the time to be on our campus. For them, I often wish it were other than what it is: crumbling staircases gated off forever; projector bulbs burnt out two weeks at a stretch; water dripping into trashcans through unrepaired roofs and crumbled ceiling tiles. Our college is committed to repurposing a disused hospital building and a long-vacant middle school. The town needs for both of these things to happen and I'm proud that we've taken them on, but the renovations are always going to be completed next year, and this year we all live with the ghost-town feeling of broken windows and dust and the promise of renewal just around the corner.

In *A Room of One's Own,* Virginia Woolf was writing of the founding of women's colleges in England when she said, "To raise bare walls out of bare earth was the utmost they could do." Her foremothers' fundraising was a stark contrast to the centuries of tithes, treasures, and endowments that flowed to Oxford and Cambridge. Newnham College at Cambridge was established in 1871, and, lightly fictionalized as Fernham College in the essay, it is a humble, single-dormitory affair that allows the female teachers and students to cling to the edges of Oxbridge life. In the century since Woolf wrote, Fernham has made up some ground: Newnham's endowment now stands around sixty million dollars.

It was 1896 when the bare walls of Suomi College were raised here in the Keweenaw as a Finnish-language seminary for the children of miners, but no one has ever poured such treasure into our foundations. We are confronted each day with such a grinding, yawning list of unmet necessities that any luxury must be second-guessed. But Woolf's essay, with its richly detailed treasures and luxuries of Oxbridge, speaks to their importance. Woolf can be flippant at moments, as when she declares of the dinner at Fernham that "the lamp in the spine"—that "rich yellow flame of rational intercourse"—"does not light on beef and prunes," but she is deadly serious about wishing for female scholars "the urbanity, the geniality, the dignity which are the offspring of luxury and privacy and space." Luxury, privacy, and space are resources afforded to some students, but not often to mine. When do my students get to be treated as if they are treasured, the chosen sons and daughters of a proud inheritance? And if this feeling of being courted by the world is out of reach, if the ceiling tiles and roof repairs are always next month, can they at least have some books?

I became an English teacher largely out of a love of books and reading. I then found myself in the position of evangelizing for, or, worse yet, enforcing the reading of books. We cannot have a conversation about a book until a student has read it. Many students may not read it until threatened with a quiz. So I became a quiz writer and learned to wear authoritarian scowls. Behind my scowl, it's a morally-compromised agony for me to fail students on reading quizzes and other assignments when they did not have the means to do the reading. Students are often sheepish about missed assignments and ashamed at the financial component of the problem. I learn to keep an eye out for the student with no book in their hands.

There's some irony that it's the English professor fretting over this. I don't use anthologies, so the most expensive text I ever assign, bought new, might be twenty dollars. It's rare for one of my classes to have a sixty-dollar book tab, and even that is a far cry from a biology or business textbook, which can cost upwards of two hundred dollars. Because it's in my nature to fret over these things, I also know that the price tag isn't the same for all students. Students without credit cards often can't shop for cheap used copies online, but they can put exorbitantly priced new books on their student account at the bookstore, to be paid up when the student loans come in.

Textbook costs are a trap. They present an opportunity to wreck your education that catches poor kids and not wealthy ones. It's not just access to cash, either. Familiarity with the norms of collegiate life matters, too. High schools provided books, so why would a student assume they will need to arrive on campus with several hundred dollars in hand just to buy a fighting chance at passing their college classes?

Williams College, my own Oxbridge, had this figured out long ago, or a remarkable group of its alumni did. The college's class of 1914 graduated into the teeth of World War I, and just six years later, raised funds to establish the Class of 1914 Library in memory of the seven members it lost in the war. The library has lent textbooks to students in need ever since, and in the course of its hundred-year existence, has grown to have a building, a librarian, and more than thirty thousand volumes. What's more, I don't think any of us realized at the time that this library was a singularity, unique in the nation's higher-education landscape. The wrap-around nature of student support was so thoughtfully designed that we were not surprised that there would be help with textbooks.

I set out to make a modest start in the same direction. I enlist the help of a graphic design student for a logo and the Student Senate for volunteers. The art student delivers a clean, lovely logo that depicts a book open to a facing page with the scales of justice on one side and the words Textbook Justice Library in a bold, serifed font on the other. The student representatives and I draw up a schedule of the classes on campus and visit all of them to announce the new initiative and make our pitch for used book donations.

When we visit the classes, we tell the students that every one of them deserves the books they need to succeed. We ask students and faculty to donate spare books to the project so that we can place them on reserve in the library. This process dodges publishers' interdiction against entering textbooks into library collections and lets the students who need books check them out and keep them all semester long. I've been adamant on this point: I don't want low-income students tethered to a library desk, a three-hour loan, a book that can't get on the bus with them when the team goes out of town.

JCPenney donates some boxes from its holiday store display, since corporate sent far too many decorations to fit in our undersized, dying local store. The boxes are three-foot cubes in Christmas consumer red—no, make that Communist red—and make perfect book-drop stations. My student with the threadbare pants is one of the first to walk up with an armload of books to donate. This is the most Yooper thing. Something is broken and we make the repair from the resources at hand. We make do.

2017

December
Grandbaby

"I don't care if the daddy's a mountain lion, I'm going to have a grandbaby!"

I share the news with Masha by sending her a package with several beloved books inside, including a copy of Barbara Kingsolver's *Prodigal Summer* with a post-it placed in one of the late chapters, a window cut into it to frame these words from Nannie Rawley. I borrow Kingsolver's words because I am still finding my own, looking for the ways to say: My kid's alone in this; I'll support her; I'll rejoice with her.

Like me, Kingsolver's Nannie Rawley would come by her grandbaby by way of her partner's daughter, a fictive kinship bond, by which I mean not a bond that's false or made up but one that is all the more precious for being co-invented and self-made.

Nannie's remark fits the daddy involved in both Kingsolver's story and ours, a young man who does not live nearby and whom our daughter Heliena now seems to know with sudden, perfect clarity was never meant to be a partner to her.

The mother-to-be in Kingsolver's book, Deanna Wolfe, is an independent and driven wildlife biologist who has always fired my admiration. I love her for her self-sufficiency, for living the lone wolf's life that I, a biology major turned English professor, once imagined for myself, and because the character's rich ecological consciousness, a unique mixture of awe for what is around her and mourning for what's been lost, feels like a life-altering guide for how to see the world. I fell hard for Deanna and identified with her hard, too: her mind, her career, her independence. Her determination to work to protect the natural world and her contented childlessness made me feel seen. Early in the book, when someone asks her about not having had children (as people will always ask women), she merely declares, with self-acceptance, "I'm not all that maternal."

And then the book, with its relentless drive toward life, goes ahead and makes her pregnant and glad about it. It's often struck me as a measure of Kingsolver's artistry that she pulls off that move without making me throw the book across the room.

I give Kingsolver a pass for this little piece of biological determinism because in its other plotlines, this book pays such good attention to the rich and diverse ways we make families: by choosing sisterhood, by choosing adoption, by loving our step-children, by stepping up as a grandparent. Even as Deanna's particular reproductive fate seemed to whisper crudely, "Biology is destiny, woman," these other plotlines speak of something more expansive: Human beings will find their greatest happiness by investing in this world and loving children, however they may know them.

After many years of defending my right to make non-reproductive choices against the expectations of others, there is something particularly hard about watching biology take such a sudden, outsized role in my daughter's life. I wanted for her the same sometimes dearly-won privilege I have had of making my life accord with my plans and wishes. Worse yet, I had assumed she would have that luxury. Heliena is a young woman who projects such strength and determination in all settings that, I'm learning belatedly, even those of us closest to her can sometimes mistake a planless free-fall for swift deliberate action. She'd tripped and fallen into life in the Upper Peninsula in June, had been living with us and taking a third crack at her senior year of high school. We'd hoped she was righting the ship when she was, in truth, continuing to drown.

She breaks the news of her pregnancy to us the week after Thanksgiving. Shawn and I walk around in a fog of shock and fear. I've got no roadmap for this phase of parenting. My parents never even had the sex talk with me. We didn't need to talk about it for it to be unthinkable.

A friend sees the overwhelm in our eyes and reassures us that this baby must be in God's plan, and wouldn't be on her way if she wasn't supposed to be here. I want to ask our friend if God's plan would look so good on her own teenaged daughter.

There are friends who gather around us and win my eternal gratitude. One of my colleagues helps Heliena navigate applying for Medicaid and WIC benefits, breezily pushing past the specter of welfare shame by announcing, "I'm a socialist. I think everyone should have this." I'm given hope by a pair of star students who are also young mothers. One is a sociologist with an infant at home who won't sleep unless he's held. She passes the time she's pinned under the baby by doing her course reading months in advance. The other student, Dana, is an English major who chipped away at her degree part-time for years until her son went to kindergarten. Dana walks me down the hall one day after class to tell me that she had needed to have her son in order to finish growing up. She gives me this wisdom and then she cares for me and this daughter of mine she's never met. She crochets a rainbow baby blanket that will become baby Jozie's favorite, and, two years from this moment, Dana, graduated, an assistant librarian, will fill a corner of the university library with kids' toys. The toys and Dana's understanding welcome and affirm Heliena on the days Jozie has to come to campus with her during her first semesters of college. While I spend many nights lying awake in terror, fearing Shawn and I will find ourselves insufficient for our daughter's needs, so many good things are growing.

Somehow, I never doubt Heliena's ability to step into this role. I know her fierce strength and steadfast capacity for love. I have real reservations about myself as grandparent material, though. I'm young in my career grind, pushing toward tenure; I won't play the role that my father's mother played when I was a child, watching me each day so my parents could work. And even were my days designed for such a contribution, I've known all my life that my nerves are not. I'm cut from the same cloth that made my own mother a desperately unhappy stay-at-home parent. Meeting my girls in their teens, I stepped smoothly over all questions of self-sacrificial childcare and straight into relationships that were deeply and immediately satisfying, ones that mirrored, to some degree, the relationship my mother enjoys with her own adult children, the happy far shore of her turbulent years of child-raising.

Watching my mother take my girls to her heart has been one of the many pleasures of being family together. Navigating the challenges and celebrating the successes of parenting has invited me to pick up the phone and call my own parents more often because I know I'll find a cheering section at the other end of the line. There has been so little time to settle into these new roles. Shawn and I have been married less than five months, and my parents have just begun telling people that yes, they have grandchildren. What will it do to this precious new family constellation to tell them that our nineteen-year-old is about to add a great-granddaughter to it? With my entire family due to arrive at my house for Christmas in three weeks, I'm going to have to share the news.

And here I learn one of the most precious lessons of my adult life: Sometimes you can ask for exactly the support you need. You can call your mother and say, "I have something to tell you, and I need your love and understanding and support. Can you give me that?"

If you are not in the habit of asking for this kind of support, you can even write it out on an index card and practice it with a friend first.

And sometimes your mother may say, "Yes."

Sometimes you can even receive all those things. Grandparenthood is a fertile ground for grace. Sometimes so is daughterhood.

And so we gather, a Dekkermoot. My parents, my two brothers, one sister-in-law, and a terrier called Radar. My parents cat-sit for one of my friends in her cute downtown apartment. My brother and sister-in-law and Radar take the big bedroom, and Shawn and I bunk next to my brother Franklin on mattresses tossed on the living room floor in front of the wood stove. We ski in sub-zero windchills and play board games. I bake my way entirely through twelve pounds of flour, three pounds of butter, and two and a half dozen eggs. We walk the snowy and quiet streets to the grocery store for more. We celebrate in my crowded-to-bursting house as the winter howls outside.

In two Christmases, we'll all be together once again at my parents' woodsy home in West Virginia. Baby Jozie, whose arrival we awaited with such fear, will be among us, her blonde hair in two pigtails like antennae. She'll wake up early to tear the kitchen apart and then have breakfast with her doting great-grandparents, who are glad to have the time alone with her and quickly learn to tie the cupboards shut. She'll read a book about dogs with my father, crying, "It's Beckett!" whenever she turns the page and sees a border collie. This tendency to recognize and speak about and to all of the animals in her orbit will make me want to scoop this child up and introduce her to the whole, wide world. In the end, Jozie herself will teach me what kind of grandmother I can be: one with picture books and puppies, ponds and pony rides and paints.

Shawn and I listened to Kingsolver's book together, once. Months afterward, he said to me, "I wonder how they're all doing, with the goats," and I was mystified until he elaborated that he'd been thinking of the characters in *Prodigal Summer*: Lusa with her goats, her niece and her nephew on the Widener farm, and Deanna Wolfe and Nannie Rawley and the baby, surely born by now and growing up amongst the apple trees. I've entertained such drifting thoughts myself, wondering what these characters are up to. By concluding her novel just as its multiple threads of narration seem about to unite, Kingsolver leaves you with that sense of continuation, the near-inevitable events about to find fulfilment. I used to dwell on whether Nannie was about to find an unlikely late-life romance with her neighbor or if Deanna and Lusa would become dear friends. I find that I'm also sure, now, that Nannie is enjoying her grandbaby just as much as I am.

2016

January
Raccoons and Salmon

"A raccoon is a nice animal?" asks Chiragee. She's looking at me uncertainly across my desk.

I suddenly appreciate how utterly North American Mary Oliver's poetry is. Chiragee's is an understandable question, given the way Oliver treats her raccoons—"silvery, slumberous." What if this "gray dreamer" was your first raccoon, his tiny paws on the riverbank spreading "the myths of the morning" in the delicate hieroglyphs of his tracks?

I remember how, years ago, a British friend asked me with rising agitation, "I don't get it. Is a raccoon a cat or a dog?" It struck me then, as it strikes me now, what wonders we grow up so inured to.

Oliver's poetry works in implicit contrast to our daily underestimation of the world. When I teach "Raccoons," I strive to help students recognize how Oliver's art asks us to see the world anew. I solicit students' usual associations with raccoons. In response to Chiragee's question of whether a raccoon is a nice animal, I supply some of the things her classmates said on the day she was absent. Raccoons come out at night and raid trash cans and rampage in campsites. If you see one in the daytime, it might have rabies.

She is a nursing student and nods her head gravely when I mention rabies, weighing contagion against awe. "Ah. It can give disease."

I run a quick Google Image search for raccoons and proffer the laptop screen. We match the images to Oliver's descriptions, breathing back into the raccoon a little of the wonder that the specter of rabies has just foreclosed.

We turn to the next poem. When I teach "The Fish," I can usually count on some sportsman or woman to say, with a glow of pleasurable recognition, that the fish is a salmon. This poem runs on wonder, too, inviting us to marvel at how the salmon can trace this river to its tributaries and choose at every branching the path that leads to her own birthplace.

Outside my office, the wind blows fine snowflakes in white swirls across a landscape of waist-high drifts. Where Chiragee grew up in Anand, India, it doesn't snow, but here the winter will last through April at least. This colorless season and its muffled sunlight feel a long way away from the dry winters and monsoon summers of Western India or from the brightness of a summer salmon run.

I try to give her the ecology: how out of the great ocean, out of all the rivers, and all their tributaries, the spawning salmon ascends against the current, against all odds, to the place where she began life as egg and alevin and fry. But even to know her lifecycle is not enough. A salmon's journey has meaning beyond the reproduction of one fish: it speaks to an intact watershed, unsevered by dams. Her life makes one piece, together with the other members of her species, of an abundant spawning run. Five such species together make the succession of spring, summer, and autumn salmon runs, the resource base that fattens grizzly bears and enables the lifeways of the people of Alaska and the Pacific Northwest.

Up in Alaska, a land I know only by legends of ecology, anthropology, and Klondike gold-rush literature, my brother works for the Fish and Wildlife Service to restore streams and give them back their salmon runs. My eyes are misted after I finish telling Chiragee what a salmon is. I do not use Google this time. All the orange-fleshed fillets or silvery leaping fish will not show how a salmon is three hundred miles of open stream and ten thousand years of human dependence on the earth's bounty.

In contrast to most of my students, Chiragee needs no gloss for Oliver's slightly archaic simile, seeing the fish as like the "body / of any woman come to term." Chiragee plans to return to India after her graduation and work as a neonatal nurse in a rural clinic.

A smile breaks across her face and she says, "It's quite deep. It's quite lovely." She tells me of how a mother's joints are altered by carrying a child to term. I had not thought to see the poem's "shaken bones" so particularly. I'm grateful.

I have never known what to make of this sudden turn in Oliver's poem, its final pivot to the celebration of the trans-species feminine strength to give life, one that transmutes the fish's upstream journey into a labor agony.

I have never been, will never be, that fish. I have a fraught relationship with ecofeminism when it indulges in gender essentialism, valuing both women and earth for supposedly sharing core qualities of nurturance and fertility. I have been living with this poem for years now, as, one after another, my friends have embarked upon their upstream journey against mortality, their very skeletons changed forever by the life they have nurtured within, their own lives brushed by possible deaths with names like placental abruption and preeclampsia.

I have never felt the need to test the fierce waters of those streams, but now, at thirty-two, there are some things I finally understand: what it is to tremble with the desire to see my family circle widen; what it feels like to make a life by making love. It's not my unborn children I see in my lover's eyes, but together we practice an embrace that may someday hold his daughters up and shelter them from life's storms. I see my other children, too—unmet, perhaps out there somewhere, already born, already needing us. In each other's arms we practice flinging open the doors to our hearts, a daily prerequisite to parenthood.

Sometimes my bones, too, feel like cages of fire. How can one body hold so much love and so much need? I know what it is to shake with the hope that my children will let me love them.

Our younger daughter is like a wild pony, sensitive and flighty. I hold out my hand, speak words of praise, am grateful when I can smooth her forelock, walk her over some new threshold. Loving her is like having a chickadee perch on your shoulder, a hummingbird sip nectar from your palm, the enchanted inhalation and inheld breath.

For several days after I meet with Chiragee, my browser remains open to the pictures of raccoons. Row on row, the whiskered, bandit-masked faces stare out at me, turning their round ears, presenting me with their hand-like paws. Their velvety coats flow over their round backs as if holding caught moonlight. They ask me if I did right to supply those ordinary, negative contexts for raccoons. Perhaps I did not. I am grateful for every striped-tailed washer bear, every miraculous promise of this world.

2020

January
On the Town

Midwinter cold. Deep snow. Sundown at five. While I usually find this season a joy, I am not immune to the occasional bout of cabin fever.

Our usual evenings at home go like this: check on our daughter's homework list; make dinner; eat dinner; chase homework assignments; finish lesson preparation. And then, finally, I build a fire in the woodstove and doze off with my husband on a mattress by the stove, a book on my chest and a dog on our feet. Later, we wake, choke the fire, climb the stairs to bed, dive in and hold each other close under cold blankets. Our nights are a warm-glowing drowsy counterpoint to days so full of demands that they leave me feeling shipwrecked and gasping.

One rare Monday evening, though, with dinner eaten and everyone ready for the morning ahead, I take a wild hare to go out for a drink. Not at the Monte Carlo a block from our house, god bless it, with its low ceiling, dart boards, wobbly formica tables, and two-dollar beer specials. This is a going-out urge.

One of my co-workers once joked that getting dressed up to go out in the Upper Peninsula consists of picking a clean-looking flannel up off the floor. My husband does indeed reach for his good flannel and a nicer-than-usual pair of jeans. I yield to whimsy: a treasured black lace dress, an antique paste choker that glitters at my collar bone, red lipstick, and—it's eight degrees out, after all—black over-the-knee boots. I briefly consider topping the look with my battered red parka, but then I dig my long wool overcoat out from the back of the closet.

The snow on the front walk squeaks underfoot as we walk to the car. We cross the bridge into Houghton and head for the Continental Fire Company. A nineteenth-century fire hall turned bar and restaurant, the beautiful two-level space is full of exposed brick and I-beams, industrial chic come home to a mining town. On a Monday night, the live music stage is silent and the space is empty of patrons. I cross the room on my husband's arm.

The bartender can't place us—likely due to my outfit—and asks if we're from out of town. One of my former students is bussing a table behind me; another is working in the kitchen downstairs. "Just Hancock," I answer.

I order a seven-dollar cocktail, something complicated with gin and a curl of lemon peel floating in a champagne glass. We pull tall stools close together at the corner of a long table. The first sip is heavenly. As I settle my wallet in my coat before draping it over a stool, I feel two slippery pieces of paper in the pocket. I pull them out. They're boarding passes dated April 2015, from Hancock to Chicago and Chicago to Boston. It's a vertiginous moment, realizing that I have not been in this coat in almost five years.

Once, I had agonized over this coat. I had acquired it during my last year in graduate school, wanting something sleek and formal to wear over interview clothes on snowy campus visits. I was acutely conscious of the faint feminine puff at the shoulders, hating it for undermining my masculine-leaning pantsuits and oxford shoes. But the price was right, and I was then so pressured and self-conscious that I could have found something acutely embarrassing about any coat.

I came home from the interview, hung up the coat, took the job, and here I was. Despite lobbing the occasional resume out into the world and sitting for a handful of phone interviews, I have not put on the interview coat in five years. I have a home, a child in high school and another nearby needing a hand with our grandchild and her own young adulthood. I have friendships, projects, professional investments, and a martial arts studio. It adds up to an entire life that seems increasingly impossible to uproot.

I chat with my husband, our faces close together in the empty bar. Then I put on my coat, which, though still ruffled, rests lighter on my shoulders without the burden of desperate job seeking. I'm ready to go out into the cold night and home to a warm fire. This seems like everything.

2018

February
Gun of Innocence

In early February, every day is startling, hurt-your-face cold. With casual, steady snowfalls of a few inches a day, we pass two hundred inches of snow for the season. While I'm herding Mackenna out into the darkness to go to school, I harness the dog and pause to smear my face with a tube of thick sunscreen against the windburn and frostbite. As I drop her off at eight, the sun is finally beginning to rise, revealing a sky of thick, unvarying gray felt. This is what my co-worker, writer Laurie Anderson, refers to as February's death shroud.

It's my third north country winter, and I have made an uneasy peace with the shroud. Every morning, I take vitamin D with my coffee and take Beckett skijoring between the high school drop-off and my first English class. In this cold, the snow is so powdery and dry that it sifts over my skis like wisps of cloud and Beckett doesn't need booties. He is as immune to winter doldrums as he is to views. He takes pleasure in his own muscular exertion, in the trail just under his feet.

After ten days with temperatures in the single digits, Lake Superior succumbs. There is eighty percent ice coverage. I begin to wonder if wolves will walk to Isle Royale again, engineering their own conclusion to years of local debate over introducing additional wolves to bolster the flagging and doomed population there.

The freezing of the lake vanquishes our cloud cover and shuts off our snow. Suddenly we have bluebird days, the sky super-saturated and cloudless, the snow glittering. Our mornings on the ski trail are drenched in gold light that slants through the trees from the rising sun. We see stars at night again, and Mackenna, ever the sky-gazer, takes long walks with the dog after dinner, enjoying the star-dazzle. Sometimes we live in such an idyll.

On February fourteenth, a shooter at Marjory Stoneman Douglas High School in Parkland, Florida kills seventeen people. Douglas' name was once synonymous for me with her book *The Everglades: River of Grass*; now for all of us it's synonymous with death.

The following day, a student at my daughter's tiny high school enters a classroom and threatens the teacher and students with a school shooting.

The threat occurs before eight thirty. By ten it's the talk of the diner downtown, but I don't know this, because I'm teaching in my own classroom less than two miles away, not gossiping over coffee and toast. Police and school officials determine that the student is unarmed and that the execution of his classmates is not immanent. They wait until the end of the school day to tell the families, sending us an e-mail referring to the threat as an "unfounded rumor of an incident which threatens the safety of our students."

After school, I have the following conversation with my daughter:

"So, aside from the threat of massacre, how was your day?"

"Pretty ok."

She tells me about her math quiz, a speech she gave in English class, a song she's working on for a solo competition. All this aside from being threatened with death.

She was not raised to expect safety. She has already checked her classrooms for nightlocks—pegs that can secure a door to the floor—and windows she can fit herself out of.

She's taken these measures, but I think she and I are both more occupied with whether she's passing Geometry this semester, whether she has all her Chemistry homework done, whether she will decide to take the choir trip or go to a martial arts tournament next month. We are so confident she has this month and this semester and a future about which to make decisions.

Many parents keep their children home on Friday. We don't. I don't even get angry until halfway through the day, pattering with my students, many of them Hancock alumni, about how the school administrators denied us parents the opportunity to decide whether our children should spend all of Thursday in a school under threat of a massacre while they searched for weapons and for words to minimize what had just occurred.

The situation tickles my sense of the absurd and I take an ironic distance, an ability to laugh at the terrible and intolerable circumstance. The result is much the same as if I were reassured: I keep rendering up my daughter to this unspeakable, unsafe world.

In the wake of school shootings, some minds spring toward defending the castle: toward metal detectors, school police officers, arming teachers, or, more plausibly, allowing teachers who are already trained to bear those arms into their classrooms. Both my husband and Andrew Pollack, who lost his daughter, Meadow, at Parkland, are of this view.

I resonate instead with the Parkland survivors like X González and David Hogg who want to see more restrictive gun laws regarding gun purchasing, background checks, and high-capacity magazines. I'm with the peacenik teachers who want to do their life-honoring educational work without an instrument of death tucked in their waistbands. I'm with everyone who worries about what armed teachers and more police in schools mean for the safety of students of color already facing the yawning mouth of the school-to-prison pipeline.

With my letters, phone calls, postcards, and petitions, I push one way. With his NRA membership and efforts to educate his younger friends in responsible gun ownership, my husband pushes the other. It seems to me that the Parkland shooter had sufficient firearms safety and marksmanship training on his NRA-sponsored school rifle team. Our little family is at cross purposes, like our nation. On March fifth, the Florida State Senate passes an incoherent compromise, raising the gun purchasing age to twenty one, banning bump stocks, funding more school resource officers, and allowing some teachers to carry guns.

In her poem "Gun of Wishes," Vievee Francis articulates an American ideal: a "gun you can carry anywhere / and no one minds your gun of good intentions." My husband is a fan of the idea of "constitutional carry," meaning he dreams of a land where citizens may carry their handguns, concealed and permitless, across state lines from coast to coast. Francis' poem unmasks this facet of American exceptionalism, a collective dream of a land where violence or the tools of violence can be protective, redemptive, and regenerative. My husband carries a gun of good intentions; he waits in all solemnity for a day when he might need to use it to protect others. We both hope that this detail, dropped into the story of our lives like Chekov's gun, will disappoint the tidal pull of narrative and remain forever unused.

Francis, born and raised in West Texas before becoming a long-time resident of Hamtramck, an enclave of Detroit, has bridged and understood American gun cultures—hunting and handgun—as I'm only just beginning to. She sends it up, all of it:

> Gun of innocence—that's the gun
> for me—one that takes out the enemy
> with bullets of care.

I saw Francis perform this poem once, her voice a rising chant that filled the auditorium, an incantation that nonetheless asked its listeners to break the spell. Violence is just violence. There are no bullets of care. Go armed or go naked, this world is sometimes too violent to be borne.

2018

February
From Mea Culpa to Me Too

I am teaching Sherman Alexie's collection *The Lone Ranger and Tonto Fistfight in Heaven* in my Native American literature class the week the Alexie sexual harassment scandal breaks. Feeling as if I must come clean by acknowledging these developments, I photocopy the *Jezebel* article, much of which is just screen caps of Litsa Dremousis's Twitter feed. It's less an article than the echoes of a blown whistle.

I fear the pall that the allegations will throw over our eighty-minute seminar, so I write "Jezebel" mysteriously as the fourth and last agenda item for the day. By postponing the inevitable, I put myself in the position of dissembling, of running the first hour of this class as if all is normal. We begin, as has been our pattern for this book, with making little plot maps on index cards for each story we have read, seeking to understand their mechanisms of climax, resolution, and revelation.

Then we take the cards for all the stories we've read and sort them into piles or continuums. If this whole ritual sounds like thinly disguised plot review, you are not far off: sometimes even my upper level English classes feel like an exercise in dragging reading comprehension out of half the class by sheer force of will.

But this kind of slow, deliberate tracking of connections yields insights that my most voracious and adoring previous readings did not. Just last week, thanks to our index cards and chronologies, I arrived at a new theory, aligning details that had escaped me on all those other readings: Jimmy—James Many Horses from "The Approximate Size of My Favorite Tumor"—is the baby James from "Jesus Christ's Half-Brother is Alive and Well on the Spokane Indian Reservation," the child thrown onto his head from the window of a burning house by his father, Frank Many Horses, and raised by the man who almost caught him. I didn't know it was possible for my love of either story to increase, but as these two stories snapped into alignment, they both lifted my heart a little more. In "Jesus Christ's Half-Brother," the narrator walks an ambiguous line between fatherly pride and delusion. He maintains faith in his son James' prescience even after years of muteness suggest he has been terribly brain-damaged in his fall. When the father claims that James finally begins speaking at age six, the other characters and the reader don't quite know whether to believe it. Bring the story alongside "The Approximate Size of my Favorite Tumor," though, and the father's faith is proved merited. Jimmy's inability to shut up is not just a fatal and marriage-destroying flaw but a miraculous gift wrested from the world's cruelty.

After last Thursday's elation, here I am on Tuesday with the *Jezebel* articles stacked guiltily facedown on my desk behind me. After we finish the plot maps, we work together to sort the cards. I have tried to come up with a few new prompts for each meeting, asking things like Who is narrating? What's the overall chronology? and Which stories are most hopeful?

Today, one of my students offers the question, "Which ones have female characters?"

We bend over the cards. Strong and well-developed female characters like the aunt in "The Fun House" or Norma in "The Approximate Size of My Favorite Tumor" and "Somebody Kept Saying Powwow" are rare, but women do at least appear in most of the stories.

I propose we try the Bechdel Test: does this story have two female characters who have a conversation about something other than a man?

Not one story passes.

Now I get an inkling of it: perhaps Alexie was always just as advertised. The male narrators and main characters in *The Lone Ranger and Tonto Fistfight in Heaven* are alcoholic, emotionally inarticulate when it matters, and occasionally terribly cruel.

In the story "Amusements," the narrator, Victor, places an incoherently drunk Spokane man on a roller coaster and leaves him vomiting under the gaze of laughing white carnival-goers and hostile security guards. The story ends when Victor flees into a hall of mirrors and feels the sensation of "the folding shut of the good part of [his] past."

Victor knows he is lost to himself because he saw the man in need of care and betrayed him instead. Somehow this clarity of self-reflection produced hope in me and my students that Victor will find his way back to goodness and become the man he knows he could be.

Alexie's creation of a character capable of such self-conviction allowed us to imagine that Alexie lived in that goodness, but he never promised us that, did he? I am reminded of Fuckhead, the narrator of Denis Johnson's famous short story "Car Crash While Hitchhiking," who turns to the reader at the last sentence, and, in the place where the narrative structure begs for a moment of revelation, tosses out, "And you, you ridiculous people, you expect me to help you."

I have been this ridiculous person through more than a decade of teaching and loving Alexie. (I nearly deleted this metonym, this habit of writing "Alexie" when I mean "Alexie's work," but I really do mean I loved Alexie, don't I?) I feel as if I have betrayed my students by holding this man and his work out to them.

At last comes the moment to hand out the article. I let the class read, and then invite my students to reflect with me upon what the revelations mean for teaching Alexie's work in the future. Should I stop? Should I replace these books with books by writers who have not exploited, intimidated, and held back female colleagues?

My students are not all that upset. They show a strong willingness to separate the work from the man, and quickly present literary-historical significance as an argument for continuing to teach Alexie's work. They are disappointed but not surprised. One student conflates the allegations of harassment with rape allegations and makes the same argument anyway, as if rape is all she ever expected from a public figure.

I leave the classroom disappointed by the discussion. I'm the only one in agony, and my students are not going to wrestle this out for me.

Alexie's fall strikes home for me because in some ways I wound up here—a white Americanist generalist who leapt eagerly to teach the Native American literature class when my dean was on the point of mothballing it—because of Alexie. He was the only Native American writer I read as an undergraduate. He led me to others. I first read an Alexie story in a fiction workshop. Void of contexts like Indigenous history or the Native American Literary Renaissance, he was presented to us as exemplary for his humor, his breath-straining titles, his pitch-perfect tonal control and ironic distance in the po-mo bad boy tradition of Donald Barthelme, Denis Johnson, and my own professor. In retrospect, it is no surprise that the advisor who slapped my ass at my thesis reading and handed me off seamlessly to the MFA director who groped half the cohort chose Alexie to be in his boys' club. The creeps all know and support each other.

As I teach source documentation for research papers to my first-year composition class that afternoon, facing me from the back wall of the classroom are colorful fair copies of the list poems my students wrote in response to a moment near the end of Alexie's *The Absolutely True Diary of a Part-Time Indian*. I was so proud of their poems; students from my other classes couldn't resist coming to read them. Now I want to tear them down. They're inspired by the moment when Junior says:

> I realized that, sure, I was a Spokane Indian. I belonged to that tribe. But I also belonged to the tribe of American immigrants. And to the tribe of basketball players. And to the tribe of bookworms. And the tribe of cartoonists...

And he goes on for fourteen "tribes." The "I realized" that starts off this passage signals a moment of revelation: Here Junior sums up what he now knows. It's a moment freighted with meaning, as in, it unfolds with all the subtlety of a fourteen-car freight train. And I was okay with that. I valued this book as a teaching text because it has so many soapbox moments, ready-made thesis statements that invite students to assemble constellations of other text evidence around them to produce readings of the novel that are rich and infinitely varied.

This passage has been making a liar out of me for years. I encouraged students to engage with it and write their own list poems in response because the poetic form is approachable and can produce such good results, but I was deeply skeptical of what's going on in the passage itself. Junior's declaration serves as a profoundly unradical moment, like the traditional marriage at the end of a Shakespeare comedy that re-contains all those wild flights of cross-dressing and female empowerment. No one ever faced genocide for loving salsa, but Alexie's list places identities with profound social consequences—Spokane identity; poverty—on par with chosen and unstigmatized categories like being a cartoonist or a basketball player or a "tortilla-chips-and-salsa lover."

There are many moments when Alexie's novel challenges its readers to confront racism, classism, systemic injustice, and cultural appropriation. My white students especially seem to experience the "tribe of" passage as an olive branch extended to them by Alexie after so much uncomfortable prodding. I mistrust it because it's placating.

And yet. Alexie's long list is a vital reminder that identity is intersectional and no one should be reduced to a single identity marker. In its eagerness to welcome everyone into a "tribe," Alexie's poem opens up space for readers to think of themselves as having multiple identities, too, and to dream of living in a world where all those identities are honored.

When I asked my students to write their own list poems in response, they shone. Using the stem, "I belong to the tribe of," they proclaimed their struggles, their heritage, their politics, their sexualities, and their dreams. I have room to teach just one novel in the two-semester first-year writing sequence, and I used *The Absolutely True Diary* because, though it's about a high-schooler, I have found no book that better mirrors the alienation and precarity of venturing into the world as a low-income first-generation college student. This book led my students to trust me and each other with sacred parts of themselves. Every year, someone came out. Every year, I learned something lovely about my students. This year, I found an unfamiliar word—philomath, lover of learning—in a student's list and learned that I belong to this fellowship, too.

Alexie called forth this beauty from my students, and all the while, he wasn't worthy of their trust. He wasn't safe.

Another conversation about Alexie's misdeeds occurs organically in my Literary Criticism class at the end of the day. Students in that class had previously read Alexie with me as first-years, had had the experience of letting Alexie help us forge a classroom community of mutual care. Their agonized groans and stricken expressions mirror my own reactions. Like me, they'd been carrying an idealized Alexie in their hearts like a friend, perking their ears to new books, new essays, news items, and radio stories about his career. And now this. They feel the news has taken something from them.

I am still wrestling it out that night with my husband on the long, dark, and icy drive home from martial arts class in Marquette. I sent him the audiobook of Alexie reading *The Absolutely True Diary of a Part-Time Indian* early in our friendship, just as it tipped over into courtship. I dropped that book in the mail like it was a guidebook to my values, a window into my life's work. I believe that education can be a ladder to our dreams. I believe that people can love each other across their differences. He took to the book as I hoped he would, laughed through it with Heliena, perhaps even understood what I meant by sending it to him. So the rural college professor courted the Detroit steelworker.

There are still fifty miles of dark road ahead of us, and the conversation churns, only roiling up new regrets. He expresses sorrow for what we would lose in Alexie as a model for craft and skill if the world turns its back on him. We are skating the thin ice of a marriage across political difference, the libertarian and the left-of-liberal. His media feed algorithms have spent the past few weeks telling him that #MeToo is a witch-hunt, but I can't blame him for wanting to snatch Alexie back from its flames. I wish I could, too. Or, rather, I wish Alexie hadn't deserved this fall. Is there any way this isn't true? he asks. I asked myself that, too. I am awaiting the investigative piece from NPR; I am awaiting a statement from Alexie, but I am not optimistic.

Our conversation circles outward into anecdote and analogy. I recall academic mentors whose behavior toward me or my peers had veered into sexual harassment. As we speak, there's an awaiting tension in me, a nearness to an abyss. I need my husband to see Alexie's behavior as a big deal. A failure to do so would feel like a failure to have my back. I feel this way even though I have continued to be polite to and even honor some of the harassers in my own life for the kind things they did for me when they weren't groping me. But tonight, after Alexie, during #MeToo, it feels important to set them all beyond the pale.

As a rhetorical technique, "How would you feel if this affected your wife, mother, daughter or other female property?" is a load of nonsense, an appeal to empathy pitched for the fatally narcissistic. But in the arc of a lifetime, a man can learn a lot from daughters. I know that the experience of raising two daughters alone helped my beloved grow into the beliefs and convictions that made him feminist in all but name long before we met.

"Would you study martial arts with someone you couldn't trust to teach the girls?" I ask.

In this shared martial arts world, we both recognize how it narrows women's opportunities when some teachers can only safely mentor men. And from those teachers, he is firm, even men should turn their backs.

And this is our answer, isn't it? A clear answer can still be a painful one. My mind is already running over my bookshelves and long lists of possible replacement texts for my first-years, but the community we will build around those texts is an as-yet unknown alchemy. I still feel trapped by my Alexie quandary, by the car and the darkness and the road that demands attention and could turn slick and perilous at any moment.

Giving up on talk, we turn to an audiobook, picking up where we left off with Louise Erdrich reading her recent novel *LaRose.* My Native American literature class read it some weeks ago, but I'm revisiting it now with him. In a few minutes we come to a passage that I think of as one of the tenderest descriptions of love ever penned. In it, Wolfred imagines how he will care for the body of LaRose, his wife.

> He closed his eyes, saw himself mixing a little mud up with his fingers. He would touch her face, smear the mud across her cheeks, down her nose, across her forehead, the blunt tip of her chin. He didn't want his beloved to be hurt in the next life, by men, the way she had been in this life.

In imagining the gesture, Wolfred maps the treasured facial features he plans to obscure and recalls a past gesture, when he strove unsuccessfully to prevent the girl LaRose's rape by the fur trader Mackinnon. In LaRose's adulthood, the two built a beautiful life despite the way the traumas of rape and family violence marked and stalked her. Wolfred's love understood, acknowledged, and was utterly and tenderly present for her trauma.

Sometimes we aim far, far too low with our lessons.

I once had a flashback in my husband's arms. I gritted my will and wished it away. It would pass; we would make love. My will and willingness remained even if my mind's eye had, briefly, betrayed me.

He took his lips from mine and asked if I was all right. I crushed myself closer into his arms, stunned, seen.

Later, afterward, cooing and wondering, I asked him how he'd known.

"I don't know. I just felt your energy change," he said.

I still think back on this incident in awe. What allowed him to feel the cold lightning of that other moment running through my blood? The empathetic leap involved nearly denies the possibility of articulability; the twice-naked intimacy of the setting makes it yet more difficult for me to write of it, but I know I must try, because I walked this earth for more than thirty years without imagining that I might be granted such care from this lover who asked for—who gently invited—my whole heart, wounds and all.

Our public conversation lags somewhere behind, out in the realm of establishing the basics of good bedroom manners like enthusiastic consent and ungrudging mutual responsibility for birth control and sexual health. It's still seeking a negative peace, a no-rape truce between the sexes. This, of course, remains vital, but it is triage work.

What if I asked more of the books I gave my heart to? Instead of hoping only to see badly-behaving characters like Alexie's Victor eloquently crucify themselves, what if I sought out texts that model good and generative relationships? I know they're out there, a stealthy canon of tenderness, a library of ideas for how to be more than self-aware of being toxically masculine. Erdrich contributes one image in *LaRose* as Wolfred lives out his nineteenth-century clerk's version of masculinity. For all that is wrong in this world, not all our forebears are monstrous. Some are tender, and we might yet learn to walk in their ways.

Coda

It was February 2018 when #MeToo broke over Sherman Alexie. That February 28th, he issued a statement painting Litsa Dremousis as a jilted ex-lover, but admitting, in regards to his many other accusers, "There are women telling the truth about my behavior." He apologized to people he had hurt, and then he went quiet.

In an interview with *Time* in 2012, Alexie was invited to ponder, "Why... are there not more Sherman Alexies?" By this the interviewer meant, why are there not other wildly successful Native American writers, a younger generation coming up behind? Alexie did not take the opportunity to praise any lesser known writer. Instead, he quickly raised and then dismissed the idea that racism in the publishing industry was to blame. "Are you kidding?" he asked. "Publishers would die if a manuscript came flying into their offices that reminded them of me or Louise Erdrich.... They would be dancing. But it just hasn't happened, and I don't know why." This swift dismissal of the talents of other Native writers came from a man who, by NPR's account, solicited manuscripts from at least one up-and-coming Indigenous poet as a prelude to soliciting sex, and who claimed to "have no recollection of physically or verbally threatening anybody or their careers," a nicety of phrasing that still admits the possible veracity of numerous accounts of such threats.

I could not continue to hold out Alexie to my students, nor ask them to buy forty copies of his book every spring, an act of collective purchasing that represents the annual high-water mark of my economic impact on the U.S. book publishing industry. It was easier, in the end, to turn my back on Alexie the man than it was to give up the *Absolutely True Diary*. I had to mourn the way my students and I lived with the book and used it to help us know each other. At some very fundamental level, this is what fiction is for: practice caring about a character; learn to care about your neighbor. This is the idealistic contract that brings me to work each day. In the end, these communities of readers are just another wider and more diffuse circle of trust that Alexie chose to violate. I wonder, as I so often do of violators, if he ever saw the beauty that was possible in that circle.

My first-year students and I now read *Brown Girl in the Ring* by Nalo Hopkinson. I try not to think of this text as a replacement for Alexie's novel. It has its own entirely different strengths. It is a brave portrayal of a teenaged mother with ambivalent feelings toward her son who comes to terms with her new role and finds power in her identity in the Caribbean diaspora. All of this takes place in a near-future dystopian Toronto plagued by drugs and healthcare inequality but enriched by resilient, cooperative, multi-ethnic neighborhoods seeking to forge a new life in the ruins of the shattered old economy. I am still learning to guide my students down the many rich avenues for discussion that this book opens.

When my Native American literature class comes around again on its two-year cycle this spring, I will teach it without Alexie. There, I don't think I'll miss him much. How could I, with a canon and a contemporary scene so rich? I will have Silko and Erdrich, of course, and also the life-affirming, intricate poetry of Margaret Noodin. I will have Rebecca Roanhorse's post-apocalyptic novel *Trail of Lightning* with its tough female monster hunter and Stephen Graham Jones' working-class werewolves in *Mongrels*, the historiography of Roxanne Dunbar-Ortiz and essays by Tiffany Midge in her inimitably titled collection, *Bury My Heart at Chuck E. Cheese's*. There will even be *Antíkoni*, Beth Piatote's contemporary play, just published in her collection *The Beadworkers*, that reimagines *Antigone* through the lens of Nez Perce characters considering the Indigenous remains in museum holdings. Who needs another Sherman Alexie when there are so many other voices, writers who remake language, worlds, and genres with a brilliance and courage that makes more room for all of us to live inside?

2018

March
Copper Dogs and Gold

My husband and I notice it the same day: a fleshy gold shimmer in the brown depths of Beckett's right eye, like a koi fish rising in a dark pond. It's not the eye that always catches veterinary attention, the left eye with its tiny fleck of blue, one of the few places Beckett flashes his secretive blue merle color. A phantom or crypto-merle border collie, he has the merle gene but looks black and white at first glance. He's tall and lanky, a classic textbook image of a border collie, though he was a Detroit stray with only his looks for pedigree when he came to me six and a half years ago.

Our vet agrees to see us the same day. The answer is not very clear but is grim nonetheless. It would take an eye specialist in Green Bay to diagnose it, but whatever the name of this tumor, the answer will be enucleation if the eye begins to give him pain. Right now it does not. We hit the ski trail together later that afternoon.

Beckett is eight this year, or perhaps ten at the outside. We are a few hundred miles short of our five thousandth mile together. I keep his running log more religiously than my own, marking in each hike, jog, and skijoring outing. I've spent these years with him logging his miles and celebrating each thousand, a ritual to celebrate the dog who doesn't have birthdays.

He has slowed down a step from last year. I knew it in November when I had to ski more carefully downhill after him, holding my skis in a thigh-burning snowplow so as not to catch him on days when the snow was icy and fast. I was already thinking that next fall might be the time to bring home a second dog. I have promised myself one breakneck, bittersweet season of running Beckett in tandem with a new dog, letting him teach the younger one to work in harness, to know gee and haw and how to bark at the mailman and open the kitchen cabinets. Will I have that tandem season? Will we reach our five thousandth mile?

When he was younger, mileage was my key to helping Beckett perform ordinary dog activities like living in an apartment or going out in public: five or six miles before an obedience class; at least three before an agility class; ten or fifteen if I wanted him to nap under a café table or be a gracious host. He was just the right amount of too much dog for me; his nervous energy and my obligation to him were what I needed to help me push the fog of depression back and get in my own mileage day after day.

Today he needs fewer miles, can be content to spend a whole day napping, watching the street, and playing fetch in the yard, though he still paces and whines with high-pitched, tooth-chattering anticipation when I reach for the harness or running shoes. Thinking about adding a second dog to the household brings me to the strange and humbling realization that now, in my permanently injured thirties, I wouldn't be able to do right by a young Beckett. We met each other at the right time, but my next dog should not be a border collie.

The weekend before we found the tumor, I attended three different starts of the CopperDog 150, a dogsled race just north of us on the Keweenaw Peninsula. As I watched each team leave the starting chute, I felt a soaring joy like a lifting sensation in my chest. My heart took flight with the teams. The curves of their backs under the harnesses were saying yes to life, and the reach of their claws and their wide-mouthed dog smiles were stretching out to grab and enjoy every mile and moment.

When I tell my brother in Anchorage about it, he teasingly reminds me that Anchorage, too, has a dogsled race starting this weekend. This is what it's like having a brother in Alaska: if I traverse the town on cross-country skis, he reports that he skied up a glacier, camped in a remote cabin, and skied down the other side; if I was at a dogsled race, he was watching the Iditarod. Driving home from the final restart at Copper Harbor on Sunday, I am satisfied and inspired, though I am wholly aware of our status as Alaska's tamer cousin. I also know it's time to re-read Gary Paulsen's Iditarod memoir, *Winterdance.*

Paulsen describes his first day on the Iditarod trail:

> I had gotten lost, been run over by a moose, watched a dog get killed, saw a man cry, dragged over a third of the teams off on the wrong trail, and been absolutely hammered by beauty while all this was happening... [The checker] left before I could tell her that I thought my whole life had changed, that my basic understanding of values had changed, that I wasn't sure if I would ever recover, that I had seen god and he was a dog-man and that nothing, ever, would be the same for me again.

Paulsen's experience is maximal, as is Paulsen himself. An evening event with him in Ann Arbor left me with the impression of a jovial Hemingway, manly, adventuresome, prone to gambling and hard drinking but kind to children. If one hundred fifty-mile dogsled races like the CopperDog are just mushers playing at thousand-mile Iditarod dreams, my skijoring is playing at what these regional mushing stars do. In many ways, I should be glad to be a miniature Paulsen.

I, too, want to put myself in the way of being hammered by beauty. I resonate deeply with his writings on his partnership with his dogs, for whom pulling is a kind of love and whose bond with their driver becomes a symbiosis. I find my greatest satisfaction with Beckett in our working partnership. He's my running partner, my pack animal, my harness dog. My husband and daughters remind me by example and sometimes out loud to stop and pet him. Six and a half years in, I still find myself bemused at his soft heart, at having the power to make another creature so happy with my touch and attention. Our big, alert home guardian leans into me until he turns slow-motion somersaults into my lap and beats the ground with his tail, nosing me again and again for just one more pat.

I'm on spring break and I spend the day after the vet visit lying on a mattress by the woodstove, reading *Winterdance* with Beckett curled warm against my body. I remember to hold him. When I finish the book, I immediately begin to read it aloud to my husband. Beckett piles in with us and we hold each other close. Tears of laughter run down both our faces as Paulsen runs his team onto a series of skunks or crashes through back yards in Anchorage at his disastrous race start.

A friend tells us that a local musher has puppies and sometimes adult dogs to retire. I look up his CopperDog bib number and go through my photographs. His small, pointy, coyote-like dogs tug at my imagination, but the second dog feels less important now than these moments by the fire.

April fifteenth brings a late season blizzard. I take my skis back out of the garage rafters. We ski the roads down to the trailhead, blowing stop signs with abandon. A child rolls down the window of a passing car to say, "I love your dog," and I say, "Thanks, I love him, too."

On the trails we make a small loop, braving moments of blinding snow driven by forty miles per hour gusts. It's good to enjoy the wild lark of it, especially now, when it feels as if any run might be the last of the season or even the last of all.

That night, Mackenna asks to go out skiing. I've put too much work on my knee already today, but I put my brace on over my tights and scramble to get ready to go with her. At the trailhead, I clip Beckett's towline to her waist and dash along at top speed behind them. They come to the first downhill and I call a reminder to bend her knees. She pops up tall, falls and gets up laughing. Skiing is still new for her, and so is this gumption: to fall and laugh and try again so easily.

She rides the next hill with more grace, zips across the snowmobile trail, shouts for the turns she wants, and we move into a pine grove where she gracefully carves a downhill curve behind Beckett, threading her way between a sapling and a foot-high snowdrift that covers most of the trail. It's a charmed moment, girl and dog working together.

She doesn't want to turn around, so we stretch our ski out long into the dusk. In the wide, straight run parallel to the snowmobile trail, I ski beside them, enjoying Beckett's body language of happiness, his easy trot, the way his ear-tips bounce jauntily with his stride, drawing my daughter easily behind him as the wind glues the blowing snow to his coat. If this run is the last, I couldn't ask for better.

2017

April
Attic Rooms

Earth Day this year dawns bright, sunny, promising seventy, even if snow is forecast overnight. I carry my seedlings outside in the morning, their first outing all week.

Little Hancock-Houghton turns out three hundred fifty people for a March for Science. As I stand at the rallying point, tears tremble behind my eyelids and I feel the urge to run away. I have allowed myself to become busy of late, walled in by daily tasks. Political reengagement doesn't feel good or even virtuous. We're marching for science, but I am afraid science is not winning. We cross the lift bridge that separates Hancock, population four thousand, from Houghton, population eight thousand. Many of those marching with us are from Michigan Tech, whose seven thousand students annually swell Houghton to nearly twice its census size. On the lift bridge, circling under it, recrossing it back to Houghton, we show ourselves to the steady stream of traffic that connects our two cities. Science draws fewer angry shouts than pro-women or pro-diversity or Black Lives Matter marches.

Even so, I am glad to retreat to the work waiting for me at home. Tansy has been choking the peony bed. I was away last summer collecting my family, and the house was vacant for some years prior to my occupancy, but the peonies have endured anyway, despite the encroachment of weeds and maple seedlings.

My childhood neighbors had peonies, and their lush, short-lived, and fragrant blooms always felt like a special gift to me because they bloomed around my birthday in the middle of June. Waiting to see when the bloom would fall each year was my accidental introduction to phenology, the science of seasonal observation. Here in the north country, I expect the blooms after my birthday. I will, in fact, carry some to my courthouse wedding on the last day of the month.

Even as I pry at the tough tansy roots, I enjoy the sharp, aromatic scent of the ferny leaves. Tansy has a sinister reputation as a poison and abortifacient, but it's known for other properties, too: as a tea, it can deworm you or your pets; steeped in bathwater, it relieves aches. I'm not about to begin brewing up pots of tansy tea, but these facts, tossed up by my memory from botanical reading more than a decade ago, are reassuring and orienting. Its yellow flowers were cheery last autumn. Someone may have wanted this plant here once.

I exercise the gardener's prerogative and grub it out. As I work, I'm listening to Claire Danes read *The Handmaid's Tale* so I can write reading quizzes on it for my summer course. I find myself regretting not having chosen a more wildly inventive Margaret Atwood book, perhaps *Oryx and Crake* with its future technologies, hybrid animals, and violent global collapse.

As I listen to *The Handmaid's Tale*, I am grateful for the warmth of the sun on my back, for the exertion of my muscles against earth and root. I pry at the ground until I bend and then break my trowel. I stand and chop the larger patches with the shovel, though I don't dare use it near the tender peonies. Eradication may not be in the cards here, but I will discourage tansy; I will tip the competitive advantage toward the peonies, their soft red stems even now raising themselves from the earth, graceful and delicately vulnerable and worthy of my care.

This gardening is a rare and necessary pleasure, a physical enacting of decisions with immediate results when so much of my life in the intellectual work of course design, lesson planning, and grading leaves little physical manifestation. Today that contrast is amplified while I listen to Atwood's Offred describe her confinement in an upper room of the commander's house: "This is one of the things I wasn't prepared for—the amount of unfilled time, the long parentheses of nothing." Intellectual work broken by physical work is one thing, but no work at all? No reading? No writing? My restlessness stirs inside me at Offred's description of her world. This novel's commitment to depicting the dehumanizing torments of boredom, of time forced into a "long parenthesis of nothing," makes for hard reading. I am acutely aware that book orders are in and it's too late to change the syllabus. So here I am, half-ducking my own reading assignment, making it more bearable by letting Danes read the book to me as I work in the dirt.

In a recent essay in the *New York Times Book Review*, Atwood reveals how she held herself to a rule when writing *The Handmaid's Tale*: "No imaginary gizmos, no imaginary laws, no imaginary atrocities." Her essay dwells on America's Puritan history and her own experience in East Berlin, and only glancingly mentions African American slavery among the many strains of human experience that inspired the events and circumstances of the novel.

It's from slavery, however, that comes the text that offers the closest historical parallel to the opening chapters of *The Handmaid's Tale*. This is Harriet Jacobs' *Incidents in the Life of a Slave Girl*, a book that describes how a woman named Linda escapes from slavery and spends seven years concealed in the vicinity of her enslavers by hiding in a small crawlspace under the roof of her free grandmother's house. I assigned Jacobs' book to my early American literature survey class with some trepidation because I worried that her seven-year ordeal pushed the boundaries of what is narratable or readable.

Jacobs' contemporaries and one hundred twenty years of later scholarship viewed the seven-year concealment as too implausible to believe.

The trail was further confused by Jacobs' artful writing, which draws heavily on the English novel of manners to describe the particular impacts of slavery upon women raised in the patriarchal Christian cult of virginity. Influenced by fiction, it looked fictive; clearly influenced by broad reading, it looked too literary to fit readers' preconceived notions of the intellectual and literary capacity of an enslaved Black woman.

I think, also, that the idea that the narrative was fiction must have been comforting to readers when, in a genteel aside, Jacobs elapses those seven years of her life: "I hardly expect that the reader will credit me, when I affirm that I lived in that dismal hole, almost deprived of light and air, and with no space to move my limbs, for nearly seven years."

It was not until the 1980s that Jean Fagan Yellin, a Pace University historian, amassed a deep archival paper trail to show that the work's unknown author (and its main character Linda) were in fact Harriet Jacobs and that the events in the book could be corroborated. In all its artfulness and all its horror, *Incidents in the Life of a Slave Girl* is a true story.

The reader has few moments to cheer during the narrative, which is largely one of suffering and dread. Had Jacobs' experience included more of the kinds of hair's-breadth escapes that make readers' hearts pound with sympathetic adrenaline, she probably would not have lived to write it. To read her story, instead, is to bear witness to how her life and her body were compressed into a long parentheses of nothing.

Our class discussions that semester, however, surprise me when they bring to the forefront a clear and quite different conclusion: this book is about a Black mother's love.

Our class is fresh from reading Frederick Douglass' *Narrative*, which testifies to the slaveholding system's premeditated attempt to destroy Black family bonds—to the point where news of his own mother's death affected young Douglass no more than the news of the death of a stranger. In telling this story, Douglass is fighting back against influential American thinkers like Thomas Jefferson who argued that slaves were incapable of higher emotions like love. Douglass unmasks how the actions of slaveholders like Jefferson produced weakened Black families that they then held up as arguments for Black inferiority.

In his brilliant book *Stamped from the Beginning*, scholar Ibram X. Kendi asserts that Douglass often fails to be anti-racist because he accepts slave-holders' assertions that there is something wrong with Black families and merely tries to tweak their argument as to the origins of the deficiency. If Black families are broken, Douglass argues, it's because slave-holders deliberately broke them. The anti-racist position is that there is nothing wrong with Black families. Anti-racism is a high intellectual bar that we should all strive to meet. Douglass' *Narrative*, in this instance, may fall short, his childhood experience of loss foreclosing for him such a position. My students' encounter with Jacobs' *Incidents*, though, suggest that here is a text that may indeed meet the criteria of the anti-racist position.

My students see Jacobs telling a different story, asserting the unfathomable depth and unbreakable strength of the love in the Black family and community. I had been hesitant about teaching Jacobs' book due to its grim, confined narrative and Jacobs' formal style, which, being modeled after highly mannerized fictional narratives of besieged virtue like Samuel Richardson's *Clarissa,* is not exactly straightforward. But when seen as a triumph of familial love, Jacobs' narrative glows differently. Secondary characters step into the spotlight as quiet heroes, including Jacobs' grandmother and other free Black family members who faced the risk of enslavement and death to conceal her. Furthermore, Jacobs' maternal love is evident in the painful restraint she exercised during those years. She writes: "Season after season, year after year, I peeped at my children's faces and heard their sweet voices, with a heart yearning all the while to say, 'your mother is here.'"

The unwritable horror of Jacobs' experience is seven years of enforced stillness, confinement to a coffin-sized loft above a porch in summer heat and winter cold. Even more than in its body-twisting effects, however, we measure this time in the growth of her children, whose mother hides above them, watching over them, powerlessly loving them as if from an afterlife.

Atwood's character fears she is as if dead to her stolen daughter, realizing, "Time has not stood still. It has washed over me, washed me away, as if I'm nothing more than a woman of sand, left by a careless child too near the water. I have been obliterated for her. I am only a shadow now. . . . A shadow of a shadow, as dead mothers become."

Atwood is on to something here: to be made as one dead to one's own children is a variety of death penalty visited upon the next generation as well as upon the victim. But the terrible punishment does not always take. Harriet Jacobs is sentenced to it, but she and her son Benjamin and daughter Ellen defeat it.

Seven years, especially when measured in the growth of a child from five to twelve or infancy to seven, is a heart-rendingly long time, enough time for a parent to become an abstraction. Before she finally escapes to the North, Jacobs allows herself one evening to spend with her son Benjamin, now twelve. She anticipates the meeting breathlessly: "I had not spoken to him for seven years, though I had been under the same roof, and seen him every day." When they speak at last, she learns that Benjamin, too, has participated in the network of protection. Hearing her cough from above the woodshed one day, he realized that his mother was hidden in the house, not safe in the North as he had been told. Without sharing his conclusion with another soul, the small boy began to keep watch for patrollers and to coax his playmates away from that side of the house, fearing his mother might cough again and reveal herself.

Five years into Jacobs' concealment, her six-year-old daughter Ellen is about to be sent to live with relatives in New York, and the family risks allowing the two to see each other. By this time, Ellen has no memory of her mother, only her family's stories. She nonetheless embraces her mother and spends the night in her arms. Ellen and Harriet Jacobs' ongoing, mutual love and ultimate reunion is as much the triumph of this narrative as their attainment of freedom.

Life could not hand Frederick Douglass back his mother as it handed Ellen and Benjamin back theirs. In our day, too, there are many mothers whom life will not give back, but there are some in whose ransom we can participate. It's become a spring term tradition for my classes to support the Baltimore Action Legal Team in their Mother's Day Bail Out. I ask students to bring textbooks to donate to our Textbook Justice Library collection while I send cash to Baltimore for each book. If we remove the flowery nineteenth-century language and the strange irony of Jacobs' self-incarceration directly above her children's heads, it's an inescapable fact that there are incarcerated women living the Jacobs / *Handmaid's Tale* nightmare at this very moment, kept from their children. They deserve to come home to their children; their children deserve the chance to defeat the Lethean death-penalty of erasure just as Jacobs' children did. There is loss enough around us. The only way I know to live with it is to try to work for a world where all captives may someday be free.

2017

May
Ramble

It's the last weekend in May and the woods are electric-bright with tiny new leaves. Spring is finally reaching the north country. Since I said goodbye to my students at the beginning of the month, my work life has consisted of meetings, year-end assessment reports, and other paperwork. It's a season when the walls of the office begin to close in, and I'm ready for a ramble.

Shawn snatches a catnap after a night shift and then wakes up to help me drop my car near the trailhead for O Kun de Kun Falls south of us near Bruce Crossing. I leave our packs in the car, and he, Beckett, and I hike just over a mile through sliding mud to see the waterfall. It's a wide, plunging fall that makes a dramatic drop down sandstone ledges. It's good to sip a little beauty together before I go into the woods alone with the dog.

There is no one in my life at precisely this moment who wants to do the sort of hiking I yearn for—to travel fast and light and long. Well, no one save the dog, who lives for it.

I leave my car at the trailhead, grab our packs, and Shawn shuttles us to the other side of my journey, forty four trail miles west. The route will allow Beckett and me to traverse the Trap Hills in Ottawa National

Forest, reputed to be the most remote and rugged nearby section of the North Country Trail. I plan to sleep two nights on the trail. The sixteen-pound daypack I'm carrying has a sleeping bag and hammock, a Pepsi stove and fuel and food. Beckett carries between three and nine pounds, depending on whether his water bottles are full. It's his strength that's letting me get by with a daypack.

When Shawn kisses me goodbye, it's an uncanny parting for him. He's been home with me for eight months now, and the moment feels emblematic to both of us. Whatever vestiges of chivalry he still carries are at war with this act of leaving me alone in the woods. Aside from a little ongoing banter about satellite phones and emergency locator beacons, he does it without complaint, and the way he'll tell stories of this moment afterward speaks to a sense of pride in me as well as some complex processing of what it means to love a woman who says no thank you to his protective impulses.

I'm going to the woods to be with the spring flowers, but also because I believe it's good for a woman to sometimes go where only a good dog can follow. I want to walk alone a while, to examine the shape of the connections I feel to this place and to my partner and family.

This is not my first solo overnight, but it's the first one where I've used this lighter gear configuration, and it's my first one since tearing my ACL. Last spring, I couldn't have done this. I was still hobbling and afraid of every jolt, and it was an easy decision to give up my northern summer to spend the months with Shawn and the girls in Detroit, helping them renovate and sell a home and pack for the move north.

A decade ago, I cut my teeth on New England backpacking on Vermont's Long Trail, laboring ten miles a day under a thirty five-pound frame pack and watching as trail-hardened Appalachian Trail thru-hikers carrying far less zoomed past me making twenty or thirty miles a day. It made me want to be stronger and travel lighter. Now it's time to find out if stronger is still possible for me.

When I reach the top of the first stiff climb about an hour later, I feel a tug of yearning for connection, for someone to hear me say, "I made the top." I dig in my backpack for my cell phone to send Shawn a text. I turn out the two pouches where it should be. I don't have any pockets to pat. I'm forced to conclude that it's still in my car at the other trailhead. I know that Shawn will worry when he doesn't hear from me, even though we weren't expecting perfect reception. But there's nothing to be done about it now. I let Beckett lead me on.

Rock and earth feel good underfoot, and my pack is light on my shoulders. White trillium are blooming in the leaf litter, and the green of new leaves and spring ephemerals is a balm to my winter-starved eyes. Seven o'clock finds us on top of another ridge fifteen or sixteen miles in, and I'm fiercely hungry. There on the bare rock, I give Beckett a snack of kibble in a generous splash of water and then light my stove and rehydrate and heat some freeze-dried scrambled eggs in the lid of my pot. I finish the whole meal with only a little help from him. We laze and linger for a few minutes more, and then begin to walk on and look for a place to get off the trail and camp. Here, as we leave the ridge, is the first and only time we see another person, a twenty-something-year-old man in a heavy pack headed in the opposite direction. We pause and chat briefly. I think of my misplaced cell phone and consider asking the other hiker if I can borrow his to send a quick text, but it chills me to think of admitting to the only other person out here for miles that I'm a woman hiking alone without one. I let the opportunity pass and hike on downhill, deeper into the national forest.

People sometimes ask me if I'm ever afraid of spending time in the woods alone. This moment is a case in point for me: given the choice between people and the forest, I'll take my chances with the forest.

Upper Peninsula twilights are so long that we make seventeen miles—twenty if you count our jaunt to the waterfall—before I settle on a little valley well away from the trail for our first night's rest. I hang my hammock low between two trees, just a few feet off the ground, and Beckett curls up to sleep below me in a contented ball, his nervous alertness sated with miles. It rains a little overnight, and it's cold, somewhere in the forties with the air moving both above and below me. Sometimes I use a thin blow-up mattress inside the hammock as an insulating layer, but I didn't leave room for such extras on this trip. I wake often and turn in the night, restless with cold and sometimes shivering.

In the morning we're both dry despite the rain, Beckett having stayed sheltered by the hammock's rainfly. I have camp broken and am on the move almost as soon as I'm awake, nibbling a granola bar and enjoying our efficiency. But today I'm rubber-legged, not used to twenty-mile days. When we top a ridge and find a sunny rock outcropping with a view into the forested valley below, I lie down on the dry rock, pillow my head on my pack, and nap. I wake up to find Beckett laying upright, watching me intently, eager to be going down the trail again.

This steady gaze of his feels emblematic of our relationship. In the three years I lived alone with him in as many towns, there was this constant: Beckett knew when I came and went, when I woke and slept and ate and ran. By observing me, he verified my existence and tethered me firmly to it. He's done the same for me just now, keeping watch while I slept on a slab of basalt at no definite point between towns. I'm not nowhere when I'm with him.

We hike into the area of the old Norwich Mine, and my imagination is fired by the interpretive signs that inform me of how the valley below me was both mined and farmed to feed miners and livestock between 1850 and 1900. It is so tempting to see the thick woods before me as original and undisturbed, but in truth they were clear-cuts and farm fields abandoned little more than a century ago.

The signs of this past are everywhere in the form of barely gated-off mine entrances and broken stone foundations. They're in the flora, too. Shortly after the trail carries me straight through a large, roofless stone building, I come upon a stretch of woods that has an endless carpet of periwinkle flowers, surely escaped from an ornamental garden bed, though no homes now stand nearby. They make a beautiful, if choking, groundcover on the forest floor. There are no trillium here.

Thunderstorms catch us that afternoon on a low section of trail, and the path disappears into standing water. I wade along shin deep, picking out the route with the trail blazes. It's safer than being on a ridgeline, but we are both soaked to the skin and are soon glad to dash through the weathered outskirts of the Old Victoria ghost town and find a modern hiking shelter with a sound roof and two bunks waiting to receive us. I'm grateful to peel off and hang my wet clothes and make myself a cup of instant coffee.

And then, almost as soon as the coffee is drunk, the rain stops and the skies clear. It's six in the afternoon. We've covered a respectable seventeen miles despite my napping. The dog's wet hair is starting to dry. We could sleep here in the shelter and then make an easy nine miles to the car in the morning, but outside the shelter the afternoon is beckoning us with beautiful sunshine and another four hours of daylight. Looking at the sun-splashed woods from the porch of the cabin, I am almost mad to be out there in them, feeling an ecstasy of love for the spring light after so many months of short sunlight rations.

I peel off my dry fleece and pants and wriggle back into my wet shirt and shorts. I'll need the dry clothes to sleep in and don't want to risk the last ones I have with me out in the wet world. After stowing them in a bag in my backpack and getting back into my squelching sneakers, we hit the trail, a glorious downhill run through the forest toward the Ontonagon River. I should be keeping an eye out for a campsite, but the downhill grade begs my feet to keep moving.

As we near the river, the North Country Trail leaves the woods and follows dirt roads instead of paths. We pick up the pace still more, hurrying to get back into the woods and find a place to sleep. The route makes for a ford below a large hydroelectric dam, and the area around it feels developed and exposed after our two days spent amid ruined and reforested nineteenth-century infrastructure.

I decide to cross the river and camp on the other side. First, I dump Beckett's water bottles so his pack will be light and buoyant if he has to swim. I plan to pause and purify water with iodine again on the other bank. Then I hitch my backpack as high on my shoulders as it will go and wade in, glad I'm wearing the wet clothes. The current, charged by the thunderstorm, is swift and deeper than it looks, swirling muddy brown. When the water comes up over my knees, Beckett starts swimming. I tuck my fingers under the front of his pack as he paddles alongside me so he won't be carried downstream away from the ford.

The depth of my misjudgment is becoming clear. The water keeps rising—to my thighs, my hips, my waist. At midstream, I feel the water hit the bottom of my breastbone. My pack isn't waterproof and my sleeping bag isn't in a dry sack.

By the time I emerge on the opposite side of the river, I know I can't sleep in a hammock in the woods in a wet sleeping bag on a forty-degree night. I have seven miles to go and three hours of daylight left to cover them in. I don't even stop to make more drinking water. Beckett shakes off and pushes eagerly toward where the trail leads back into the woods. It's about to be a distance-record day for both of us, a literal marathon, and my knee is howling at me. I push myself hard, and soon I have to chirp encouragement at Beckett for the first time to keep him striding out ahead of me.

I perform a mental trick on my knee pain, observing my legs work, seeing them take stride, and stride, and stride. It's almost as if I'm floating along slightly above and behind my body on the trail; I'm less distressed by the pain than I am proud of the ability to keep moving at a steady clip. I know I'll make it, even if I have to hike in the dark. I let myself feel the pull of home: a shower, a kettle, dry clothes, dry feet; walking in the door to hug Shawn and Mackenna and restore to them the pet I've absconded with for two days.

I'm grateful to find that the last mile of trail is lovingly maintained by volunteers who have placed boardwalks in the marshy sections. Instead of bogging and wading and leaving our footprints gouged deep into the wet earth, we stride along the boards as dusk falls, protected from the trail and it from us. The hooting of owls calls us out to the road, where I owe someone a phone call.

2018

June
Little Stranger

As we pull into the fairgrounds in Appleton, Wisconsin, we notice the climate-controlled trailer still parked along the drive. It arrived last night from Alabama, packed with dogs sprung from a county shelter where the euthanasia rate far outpaces the adoption rate. More than a hundred dogs are here today, taking their chances at finding families in the upper Midwest. The lawn is dotted with dogs running, resting, and playing with volunteer handlers. Still more dogs are indoors in the exhibit space in crates, cages, and pens. A volunteer brings us out to the lawn to meet our puppy.

She's white, with small, upright ears and a long, fox-like body, fifteen pounds with room to grow. She greets us and leans into us happily, and I gather her into my arms and ask, "Do you want to come home with us and be our puppy?" My eyes well with tears of joy. I can hardly believe it's so simple.

On the way home, with the puppy dozing in her crate in the back of the car, I keep turning to my husband and saying, "I can't believe they gave us a puppy!"

There is so much we cannot know yet—how she'll turn out true to husky nature and adore being outdoors in all weather; how she'll howl in perfect imitation of passing sirens; how she'll prove an able harness partner to Beckett and an adept hunter of backyard mice, pouncing on them in a perfect coyote arc; how she'll love every person she meets and reserve special gentleness for toddlers and tiny children, sitting down and scooting herself the last few inches into their embraces so as not to knock them down.

For now there is only the astonishing promise of her plush coat and amber eyes, the gentle trust with which she melts into our arms. When we get to the house, we carry her, cage and all, into the back yard. Beckett bursts from the back door, barking a challenge. The puppy cringes, all softness inside her shark cage, until Beckett calms and we bring them both inside. Beckett has told her in no uncertain terms that her place is on the edge of our family circle, and it will be the work of months to bring her, the little stranger, fully into the fold.

We call her Solnit, after the writer Rebecca Solnit, whose work is a continual reminder to me to work for the world I want. Rebecca Solnit has an oft quoted passage in her book, *Hope in the Dark*, in which she writes, "Hope is not a lottery ticket you can sit on the sofa and clutch, feeling lucky. It is an axe you break down doors with in an emergency." I feel in need of this fierce, active hope as I look ahead to a time in my life when I will have to take solace in the wild places all around me without Beckett's two dark ears bouncing down the trail ahead of me. My sense of the American political landscape, too, is that I will appreciate spending the next decade of my life calling my dog by a name that reminds me daily to keep on swinging the axe of my hope.

Rebecca Solnit has been schooling me in activism for a long time. Because I have a research interest in the American literature of the atomic bomb, I first knew her book *Savage Dreams* for its descriptions of anti-nuclear activism at the Nevada Test Site between 1987 and 1992. Her description of her brother, David Solnit, was a revelation for me. At the time of her writing, he was an anti-nuclear activist; today, twenty years later, he is an artist and activist who is deeply committed to the climate movement. Solnit muses:

> So many Americans seem to think that activism is an aberrant necessity brought on by a unique crisis, and then throw themselves into it with an unsustainable energy brought on by the belief that once they realize some goal or other, they can go home and be apolitical again. I always admired my brother for the steady nonchalance with which he approached his work, recognizing that political engagement was a normal and permanent state.

David Solnit's "steady nonchalance" and the cyclical, yearly pattern of activism in *Savage Dreams* introduced me to something pastoral in the pursuit of activism. The narratives of activist lives are cyclical, not linear. David Solnit's activist career arc reminds me of anti-war activists of the Vietnam era like Father Berrigan who transitioned later in life to anti-nuclear work, or Mary Austin's pivot from women's suffrage to indigenous land and water rights. For many activists, the path is lifelong. Much as with the life-yielding activities of gardening or farming, there may be a season of preparation and planting, a time of great effort, a harvest, and even sometimes a festival day, but there is no finish line nor any climactic final battle. The cycle always turns and planting comes round again. I call our puppy Solnit, then, for both Rebecca and David, and now I have (an English professor's dream) a chance to talk about one of my favorite authors every time someone says to me, "Cute dog! What's her name?"

Solnit the puppy comes with me to Literature and Gender class in the fall when we read Rebecca Solnit's essay "The Mother of All Questions." In it, Solnit strives to make more elbow room in our ideas of what it means to be a woman—or any human being—seeking a meaningful way to love and contribute in and to this world. My class has just read *A Room of One's Own*, and is ready to share Solnit's frustration with encountering the repeated question of whether Virginia Woolf should have had babies. Eighty-seven years separate the 1928 lecture that became Woolf's famous book from Solnit's essay on her.

Woolf's work has reverberated down the decades, entering the popular and the critical imaginations. In the third chapter of *A Room of One's Own*, Woolf invents for Shakespeare a fictive, "wonderfully gifted sister, called Judith." Woolf uses her as an occasion to explore the social forces that would have thwarted female artists in Elizabethan England, and to lament how little could be known of women's lives, given the paucity of records about them in that day. Germaine Greer's 2007 historiography, *Shakespeare's Wife,* seems at last to answer Woolf's wish by reconstructing the religious currents, social relationships, cottage industries, and communities that would have made up Anne Hathaway's world. In the fifth chapter, Woolf observes the rarity of literary representations of female friendship and the failure of novels up until Jane Austen's day to represent women except "in relation to the other sex." Here is the germ of the idea for the Bechdel Test, which sprang into the world as a brilliant conversation between two characters in 1985 in Alison Bechdel's comic *Dykes to Watch Out For.* It condenses Woolf's observations into a simple, three-item test for film and other media. Does the work contain two women who have a conversation about something other than a man? The Bechdel Test is nearly as old as I am, but it still breaks over readers with a stunning clarity. One might rightly think there has been vast progress for women since Woolf lectured in 1928 and Bechdel drew in 1985, but half of films made each year still cannot pass this test. And in 2015, people still want to ask Rebecca Solnit about Woolf's babies, not her books.

We examine the passage that Solnit references in "Professions for Women" in which Woolf stabs to death the Angel of the House. The angel is the feminine ideal that tells Woolf to be self-sacrificing, flattering, and deferential to men and to men's writing. The fluffy puppy Solnit roves happily from table to table as I take the plunge into the personal and ask my students if there's an angel stalking them, too, some rigid model for life that they would rather slay than mold themselves after. I hand my students dry erase markers and let them write their ideas under the wings of a dark and menacing angel that another student has drawn on the board. One young man names the idea that a man must be the breadwinner of a family. Other students offer up perfectionism, beauty standards, compulsory heterosexuality, religious expectations, the assumption that all people aim to be in relationships, and the equating of money with success.

I wish I could wave a wand and free my students from all these models they yearn to shed. In the meantime, at least we can name them, spell out the demands of this demon as baldly as Woolf and Solnit did, and then drive the eraser through them. And there's a puppy here to hug, whose furry shoulders, already broadening into maturity, are unburdened by the symbolic freight she's asked to bear.

2018

July
La Belle-Mere

I tell the waitress outside Giverny, "*Ma fille voudrait un dessert aussi*," and my restaurant French inspires several rounds of disbelief, to which Mackenna and I both insist, "*Oui*," laughing. It's not shocking that my daughter wants a dessert; the surprise, the waitress is quick to share, is that I have just revealed that we are not sisters.

I want to offer the gilt-tongued response, "*C'est la fille de mon coeur, pas mon corps.*" The words, *coeur* and *corps,* heart and body, sound indistinguishable, at least to my American ear. But I don't venture the sentence. My French language daring does not extend to punning.

There is strong social pressure to act flattered each time people find me illegible as a mother: when someone tells my husband they didn't realize he had three daughters; when the new guidance counselor at my daughter's high school asks if I'm there to pick up my schedule; and here, when the waitress says "*Bon travail!*" to me: a job well done for looking so unmotherly and so young. Now that my appearance has been scrutinized, my daughter can have some ice cream.

Parenting in public provides me with countless opportunities to decide whether to deflect or accept the congratulations that are aimed at me for appearing youthful and for living in what looks like a pre-baby body (the only body I will ever live in). My daughter and I look enough alike that strangers quickly make the leap from taking me for her sister to concluding that I am indeed, by some confluence of teenage pregnancy and/or a good face regimen, her biological mother. I always feel a stab of half-ironic guilt, as if I am appropriating the dubious gift of these bodily compliments from another, also beautiful, woman who gave birth to, but does not parent, this child.

I would rather be congratulated for doing what needs to be done or for having a wonderful daughter, yet I'm expected to be grateful to be told that I do not look the part for the most important role in my life. Women are always expected to be flattered when told we look young, even as youthfulness and underestimation go hand in hand.

Throughout my life, I have also been readily mistaken for someone who would soon, inevitably, wish to reproduce. From a young age, I knew in my bones that I wanted a family but not babies. This conviction only solidified as my environmental commitment and self-knowledge deepened. Even as a teen, I felt the expectations chafing me. I might have found more fellow travelers had I been in the "I hate children" camp of the childless, but, caught between the norm and the opposite extreme, I often felt fenced in by others' lack of imagined alternatives.

I read Dan Savage's memoir, *The Kid*, while I was in college. It kicked off a phase of reading all the gay parenting memoirs I could get my hands on, because I felt it healing something in me to watch Dan and his partner Terry swimming upstream toward parenthood against the flow of social expectations. Their stories helped me preserve parenthood as a rich and worthy dream in my mind.

One of the most memorable moments of Savage's memoir comes when Dan and Terry get on a plane with their infant son, D.J., and the gate agents, flight attendants, fellow passengers and even the captain want to know, "Where's mommy?" and "Are your babysitters taking good care of you?" and "Which one of you is Daddy?" Experiences of parental illegibility are a trope of adoptive-parent memoirs. The very first one I ever encountered, an old Reader's Digest Condensed Book version of *They Came to Stay* that I found at my grandmother's house when I was about ten, had one, too. In it, journalist Marjorie Margolies mentions on television in the early 1970s that she has two daughters and no husband. Angry viewer letters pour in about her fallen-woman status; to quell the uproar, she comes out publicly as the first single American woman to have built a family through international adoption.

Experiences like these pose challenges for the families that undergo them, but they exert a powerful and positive narrative force, creating a shared joke between the author and reader at the expense of a world that gets it wrong at first glance. I liked being in on the joke and admired these families for living their lives, damn the appearances. I suppose all this reading was good preparation for my own easily mistaken mothering.

In the worst of these encounters, people prolong their discussions of my age and appearance, probing at me or even making suggestive comments about my probable age of parturition. I was eighteen and near to graduating high school when my younger daughter was born; such an alternate history of my life would not have been impossible, though I suspect that it would not have left me with a doctorate and a still-cardable face at thirty five. But anyone who is fishing for those details does not, in my view, deserve them. These conversations sometimes take on an aggressive edge, as if the inquisitor has me pegged for a fraud and is needling me to see if they can make me retreat from the word *daughter.* In the face of such hostility, I tend to resist providing that qualifier, *step-*. My daughter does not say step-mother, so I do not say step-daughter.

I've never asked her why that isn't in her vocabulary. Perhaps it's because I was mothering her before my marriage to her father made the title of *step-mother* a technical fit. Perhaps it's because of the bad rap that step-mothers get in our fairy tales. I just know the shock of pleasure and alarm that coursed through my body the first time she shouted for my help through the house, "Mommy Carolyn!" It was just a few days after she and her father moved north to live with me, and at fifteen, she was old enough to do the choosing and the naming. In these years of living as family, the words have varied. Last Christmas, our gift tags said *Mere* and *Pere*. Shawn is often Opa, sometimes just Shawn, while I'm just Carolyn, or mother, or Mama Dos.

She brought the French words for step-mother and step-daughter home to me one day when she was assigned to create a family tree for her French class. As we pulled out of the school parking lot, I had the laughing realization that I didn't know the word for this role that I lived in.

How had I never learned it? The years of classes, the books, and, most recently, the apps, had all let me down. My high school French teacher, a treasure of a woman and a native speaker from Brittany, always used to tell us, "When you can't think of the English for a thing, say it in French." She reinforced the notion that French was a romance language in both senses of the word, made for nuances of the heart. Even if my community did tend to treat divorce as an unspeakable scandal, I grew up with peers who had step-parents whose French titles we never learned. To have or be a step-parent suggests that Plan A has somehow gone awry and you are living out Plan B; in learning the French nouns for the world around us and even for the great journeys of the heart, we neglected the words for the essential and everyday work of picking up the pieces.

"How do you say step-mother?" I asked my daughter.

She paused a beat. "I think it's *belle-mere*," she said.

"Oh, that's lovely!" I cried. "So, step-daughter . . . ?"

"*Belle-fille*."

The French language has always seemed to me stamped with the logic of women as property. *Une femme* is a woman but *ma femme* is my wife, whereas men and husbands, *les hommes et les maris*, merit two different words. It is the same for boys and sons, *garçons et fils*, while girls and daughters are both *filles*. Suddenly, though, with the gift of this new term, *belle-fille*, this vocabulary of possession seemed to have the potential to operate in reverse, in liberation. The step-daughter is made out of the gentle endearment of *belle*, and that contextual, protean *fille*, making her the beautiful daughter and the beautiful girl, a *fille* who ultimately belongs only to herself.

I went to my *Petit Larousse* when we got home and learned that the French use *belle-mere* for both stepmothers and mothers-in-law, and reserve another word, *marâtre*, for wicked and cruel mothers, biological or otherwise. *Belle-mere*, on the other hand, is flattering at first blush: the beautiful mother.

As opposed to the other mother? Perhaps it is cynical after all, a nod to the pretty young wife that many a man trades his first wife in for? I'm sometimes acutely aware of how my young face lends itself to this narrative. I surprised my husband's friends by being six years younger but having a career far away and a home into which to invite him. I wear the face of a gold-digger, but the hat of a co-provider and co-parent, even and especially for the parts of parenting that are not fun. I am sure I am the *marâtre* sometimes, since I'm the parent in my daughter's life most invested in things like schoolwork, seatbelts, safety helmets, and toothbrushes. I file away *belle-fille* and *belle-mere*, glad to have learned the words that, in an emergency, might explain us.

Traveling abroad together is a strange mixture of solitude and scrutiny. We have so much time to be ourselves alone together. There's the long flight, the restaurant meals, the poring over city maps and museum guides. Our first few nights in an Airbnb in Paris mean that there's not even so much as a concierge to say *bonne-nuit* as we come and go. Only we mark our passage in the city.

She clutches my arm to steady herself on the crowded Paris metro car. If her father were here, she'd grab him first; this is the pleasure of being on a jaunt, just the two of us. It's a long drink of the solo parenting I've been sampling when my husband works a string of night shifts or travels for a few days, the pleasurable intimacy of being necessary and reliable and sufficient to our child. She asks me how many stops until we get off the train and I show her how to count them on the map above the door and how to find the name of the train using the last stop on the line. Then I tell her that she's planning our next metro journey. I love that she reaches for me today even as I work to make her more independent tomorrow.

During my months of planning this trip, people often asked me, "Why?" or, "To study?" Perhaps the question came up so often because of my history of traveling the world on the academy's dime or because the extravagance of the trip was so out of character for me: the summer prior, I had a courthouse wedding celebrated a month later with a big sparring round robin and a picnic. So much of what we do as parents is strategic. If you clean your room, then this; if you finish your homework, then that. And I do want certain things from this trip. I want my daughter's dreams to be bigger than our small town. I want to make a promise to her and keep it.

After having this conversation in English for the months leading up to the trip, I revisit it several times more in French. On our first night in Paris, as we sit on the lawn and wait for darkness to fall and the Eiffel Tower to put on her lights, we chat with a friendly man from Nice called Rahm. He is still basking in the afterglow of the World Cup win. He is interested to hear that we will not just see Paris, but also travel the Cathar country on horseback. He asks me why I have left my husband at home. I choose not to detail our finances, and I lack the words for "allergic" or "security theater," so I settle on "*Il n'aime pas les avions ou les chevals.*" He doesn't like airplanes or horses. This provokes a gust of laughter from Rahm. "What *does* he like?" he asks. I list a few things, and then I nudge the conversation back toward Mackenna.

Of many answers I tried, the answer that felt best to me, in the end, and best for Mackenna to hear, was the most selfish one. The trip is for pleasure. Mackenna loves art, music, and horses. She's the perfect travel companion. Who else would join me on an adventure like this? *Elle est parfaite.*

We're both aware of her father's absence, but even more, I think, we feel his presence. He's there in the affection between us and even in our missing him. I fumble to explain it when I get home without sounding morbid, but this journey gives me a sudden understanding of how, now, should one of us die, we won't really be gone at all. Loving our daughter is something I do for its own sake, but it is also a way of loving him.

I encounter each day in Paris eager to see the sights but also to see what will draw her in, what she will love best. We move through the Louvre together at a rapid pace, pausing to retell each other the myths of Greece and Rome that the Classical and Neoclassical art calls up. We delight in reaching the end of our knowledge when we meet a new mythical creature, a marine centaur, who is like a land centaur except that he has a fish's tail. We meet him in the act of abducting a Silenus, carrying the sturdy, bearded old man struggling into the sea. We do not know the Silenus, either, and vow to look him up when we get home.

A few rooms over, another Silenus is also having a very bad day. He is hung by his wrists on a tree that is edited down to just the trunk and one abbreviated branch, a simple gallows.

"Is it Christ?" Mackenna asks me.

"It can't be," I say, but his ribs protrude with the same painful, pathetic beauty as they will on countless crucifixes in the centuries to follow, to the point where my visual vocabulary, too, short-circuits to Christ at first glance.

The gallery card tells us that here, in *The Torment of Marsyas,* the Silenus is hung from the tree because he is awaiting flaying after losing a musical contest with Apollo.

"It's another Silenus," I say.

It's a startling sculpture for its depiction of anticipated pain and victimhood rather than muscular, masculine heroism in motion. The tree and branch are arresting, too, in a gallery full of isolated human figures. Yet even while it's being used to harm him, the tree seems right for the Silenus. He reminds us of a Satyr, even without horns or hooves. Is that because Pan's is the only other mythic Greek body we can think of that isn't enviably muscled or boyishly graceful? We are not far off. Satyrs and Sileni both dance in Dionysus' train.

Did we see the *Mona Lisa*? Barely, from a distance. The *Venus de Milo*? Behind a crowd. But we saw the Louvre as only we two could have, wandering, wondering, mistaking, and learning.

I add Le Centre Pompidou to our Paris itinerary the next day because Mackenna expresses an interest in abstract art, but the visit does not go our way. She finds the surrealism disturbing and the penis count too high. Worse yet, the museum has wifi, so she trails me through the galleries with her nose in her smartphone, treading on my heels as she texts her friends at home.

Le Centre Pompidou seems an utter failure, but then, hunting for a bathroom down a narrow corridor between galleries, I come face to face with a familiar painting.

I know this street: a wet earth road; a large, thatched-roof building; a dark, dramatic storm-clouded sky; and a woman, blonde and aproned, standing before the building. I'd spent hours staring into this painting—or, rather, its replica—in the hallway of my childhood home. I loved the ominous sky and the sunshine riot of the texture of the thatch, echoed by the brighter oranges in the standing grass beside the road. My great aunt Eleanor was a painter. Her methods as both a student and teacher were at least as old as the Renaissance: copies upon copies. She taught art classes for more than six decades, so she produced a staggering number of copycat canvases. In some of these cases, she noted the names of the original artist on the back of the canvas, but if one is in the habit of looking at the front side of paintings, such details can fade with time. Aunt Eleanor gave her art away to friends, students, and family with a free hand, and my mother's appetite for her beloved aunt's work could be indiscriminate at times, even to the point of begging half-finished work. All of it went into frames that spangled every wall of our house. It's no wonder we displayed the painting all those years without my ever knowing it was a copy.

Here I was, face to face with the original, thirty five hundred miles from home. It's a 1933 painting by Maurice de Valminck, the Fauvist—though this composition suggests a later turn to nature. It's called *Chaumières*, taking its name from the thatched buildings. Part of the painting's enduring fascination for me had been its utility poles. Running along the road and into the distance, they disrupted my sense of the scene's setting in the agrarian past. Electricity or even a telegraph wire felt to me so at odds with the centuries-old thatch and the rural landscape that the poles seemed not to be rooted in the earth but rather reaching down from that sinister dark blue sky. Growing up surrounded by New Jersey suburbs, what did I know of lives where modernity and the past rubbed their shoulders together in such ordinary, everyday ways?

I wonder if Aunt Eleanor might have seen this painting when she and Uncle Joe travelled in France in 1959, retracing the steps of his wartime service. I feel an irrational thrill, as if I am on her trail, though the Centre Pompidou was not built until 1977. The painting was bought by the state before the war, in 1939. Even now, the gallery information includes the fact that de Valminck "took part in the propaganda trip organized by Goebbels in 1941." Were French painters who flattered Nazi occupiers sufficiently rehabilitated to line the narrow corridors between galleries in some other Parisian museum by 1959?

I don't know, but I grow buoyant at the idea that Mackenna and I are following after Aunt Eleanor; I am so grateful for the ways her life forged a path for my own. She had no children, giving the lie to the "when you have children" language of inevitability that I waded through for so many years. She doted on her nieces and grand-nieces and -nephews. Most fascinating to me of all, she lived a creative life, surrounded by sweet and affectionate community. She was the only adult in my family who didn't hate her job, and this fact above all helped set the pattern for my dreams.

That Aunt Eleanor had been to Paris had passed into family lore, but I missed the opportunity to really speak to her about it and ask her what she had seen, just as I never took the opportunity to ask her about her childlessness. To this day, I do not know whether the status that so fired my imagination was her deliberate choice or a silent, closely-held tragedy.

After the Centre Pompidou, we retreat down the block to a café for lunch. My daughter puts her phone away—another of my *marâtre* rules—and we talk happily. Our waiter keeps circling back to our patio table, chatting with us, and I am so aglow that I try to spill the whole story of the painting, my aunt (*la soeur de ma grand-mère*), and 1959. I know that I'm at the outer limits of my language competency whenever I stray from the present tense, but he's too polite to tell me that my French is garbled. When he next returns, bearing our bill and two coffees, "from me," I ask the meaning of the name of the restaurant, "Chouchou." He corrects my pronunciation, a soft "Ch" sound, not the "choo choo" a train makes, and tells me that it's his own nickname; this is his café. When he sees that the espresso-style coffee is too much for Mackenna, he returns with a larger cup and a tiny pot of hot milk. I wind up drinking the latte in the end, but we both bask in his kindness. He urges us to come back in the evening for live jazz, and I don't share with him the complex itinerary that will whisk us away from Paris for the next week.

After Paris, we take a high-speed train south and spend a week riding horseback in the foothills of the Pyrenees, going from inn to inn without a guide. We and our horses thread rural lanes and wooded mountain trails across one hundred kilometers of countryside. I carry the directions and she the map, a surrender to her self-sufficiency that takes some willpower; I only ride alongside to check her mapwork about four dozen times a day. We reach each known place on our maps, the towns and their bridges, the centuries-old fountains we open to water our horses, with a sense of relief to be found again after traversing the unknown in-between. To the people we meet along the way, we are equestrians and adventurers first, we who *faisons la randonnée au cheval.* Second, *nous sommes américaines*. Our familial tie is far from the most interesting thing about us. We simply are us, making decisions, choosing paths, drinking in the days together. As I have bragged all along, for this trip, *elle est parfaite.*

And she is. Adventure vacation carries its own hardships: ninety-plus-degree summer heat; a day we run out of drinking water; two days we must ride through forests full of dangling caterpillars; a blow to the head from a tree branch that might have cracked her skull if we hadn't lugged her riding helmet all the way across the Atlantic; the time a cyclist behind us on a road startles the horses into a run and she's caught with her feet out of her stirrups and has to hang on, hell for leather. The thing I'm proudest of and most grateful for is that she stays kind throughout it all.

After Cathar country, we have a final day in Paris. Mackenna asks to spend the spare day taking the train out to see Monet's home and garden at Giverny. I leap at the idea. It's the stuff of my childhood dreams. I had always imagined that Aunt Eleanor had seen Monet's garden because she had told me about the place, had fetched home a documentary about it from the library of the art museum she helped found and shown it to me on a sweltering Florida night in my girlhood. On this visit I learn that Monet's garden was not restored and opened to the public until 1980. Again, I don't know what France she saw in 1959, but I still feel myself picking up her trail by living out the dreams we wove together.

I spent many glad childhood hours by my aunt's side, wasting perfectly good watercolors and paper. I have never had a visual artist's skill. I turned to photography, to words, to the muscular self expression of martial arts. My daughter has the skill and the drive to improve it. She jostles for space on a bench by Monet's lily pond and settles in to sketch. The day is gently overcast, and I circle the pond, using a cheap fisheye lens to make my own impressionist blur out of the serene, underwater colors that surround us. While the garden near the house pops with tree-trained roses, hot-hued dahlias, and Mexican shellflowers in dappled magenta, the plantings around the pond are dreamy and subtle. Pale pink wild roses glow from the path margins; purple-dappled Hypoestes leaves are paired perfectly with pale purple impatiens that swim up into the vision like the sunlight sparkling on the pond under its thick canopy of drooping silvery willow boughs. I keep returning to check on her, watching the sketch grow outward from the famous bridge. Quiet awe thrills through me at witnessing her way of seeing and being in the world.

I tell my artist daughter about my artist great aunt sometimes, and like me, she's growing up in a house with art jostling for position on every wall: her own paintings, my photographs, Aunt Eleanor's paintings. I love and miss my aunt, but I don't find myself having that conventional longing, "I wish you could have met her." I think Mackenna meets her every day, in the ways Aunt Eleanor is present in all the choices I have made to be someone who lives my passions and nurtures by choice, not conscription to biological destiny. Or, if by biological destiny, only by the shared human impulse to love and care. I think that one of the lessons of this trip for me is that the ones we love will always come back to us as we go on loving.

On our last night, we wander more than a mile through Paris to the famous English-language bookstore Shakespeare and Company. My daughter's been economizing her pocket money to afford a beautiful, hardbound edition of Lucretius' *On the Nature of Things* that caught her eye. From there we meander back to Café Chouchou, as much for a destination to walk to as for the promised live music. Mackenna orders duck—what adventurous tastes she has come back out of the mountains with! More than a week has passed since our last visit, and hundreds of tourist faces must have passed through this café since then. Surely he can't remember us, but Chouchou himself is all charm, and glides over with two glasses of sparkling wine "from me." Mackenna deliberates, takes a sip of hers, and then slides it over to me, as with the coffee. The champagne glow of the evening deepens, and the parental duty of finishing my child's food has never felt so good. As we walk back, there are dancers by the Seine, and the world is incomparably beautiful, full of love and music.

In our final moments in France, standing before the passport control officer, I fear the stakes of my maternal illegibility. I break my no-step rule in favor of precision, telling her, "C'est ma belle-fille," and nonetheless the interviewer calls her supervisor over, saying—there's that phrase again—"*Je croyais que vous étaiez soeurs*!" I laugh and try to act flattered, but the introduction of the second official seems ominous. All I want is to get out of France without my daughter being detained as a trafficked minor. Switching to English, the officer gently asks her about her life, making sure she can supply details that verify that she does, indeed, live the life of a high-school student and horse enthusiast in Michigan. What's her favorite subject in school? What color horse does she ride? Where does it live? The grilling is cheerful and innocuous but gives her ample opportunity to blink for help. It's the friendliest near-international incident in which I've ever been involved.

And when it's over, they let me fly you home. *Ma belle fille* (translate those words how you will), I want something to call you that is even more beautiful than daughter—if there is such a word—that says you chose me and I chose you. But until I find that word, *daughter* will have to do.

2018

July
Labau

Something that surprises me about our time in France is the sheer number of books I manage to read despite the packed, nonstop nature of our days. I finish Percival Everett's *Half an Inch of Water* on the plane and release it to the bookshelf of our rented apartment in Paris, wishing it well and glad to lighten my load. My insomnia has followed me across the Atlantic, turbo-charged by jetlag. In addition to pre-reading my guidebook for our upcoming sites, I try to lull myself to sleep with audio tours and, when that fails, I begin nocturnally purchasing and borrowing ebooks: two memoirs of Joan Didion; a biography of Louis XIV's mistress, Athénaïs, that is a beautiful orientation to Versailles; David Downie's eclectic history, *Paris, Paris.* I throw tidbits from these readings to Mackenna during our walks or over meals together, less, I hope, from a pedantic desire to make this trip educational than from sheer delight in the glimmering jewels of history and story that these writers have given to me.

After four days in Paris, we ride the high-speed train south to Carcassonne, the medieval city that will be our jumping-in place for a five-day unguided horseback tour of the Languedoc region. On the train, I finish *The Sweet Life in Paris*, the memoir of David Lebovitz, an expatriate American pastry chef.

In Granès the night before we begin our ride, we dine alone in the hotel restaurant. Our meal includes a cheese course, and we are each served a small plate with slices of three different cheeses on it. I tell her what I've just read in Lebovitz's book about how French social etiquette demands particular rules for slicing from a communal cheese course: any slice should include the rind as well as the center; take triangles from round cheeses and long straight cuts from triangular or rectangular ones. Don't take the nose—the pointy end—of a triangular cheese; this would be rude and arrogant. Take up to three types of cheese on the first round, and go back for seconds if there is enough.

I have a storytelling aim in giving her all these details: I am working my way up to gleefully recounting Lebovitz's story of a Parisian dinner party gone wrong, when a beautiful cheese course was brought to the table, and, as everyone sat for a moment in awe and reverence, a New Yorker grabbed the knife, said, "I'll just make this easier," and reduced the entire cheese course to cubes while the other guests watched in horror. The appalling anecdote lands as well as I could have hoped: Mackenna is wide-eyed and aghast and laughing at the gauche American.

That night, we retire to our room and lay the map out across its twin beds. I read the directions aloud while she traces the turns. We will leave Granès, strike westward by trail and then by road, then leave the road and ride up into the mountains to the castle of Puivert before descending to the village of the same name. I lie awake, reading a history of the Cathars, the dissident Christian sect who were persecuted to extinction in this region by the Catholic church in the thirteenth century, and wondering if we will find all the turns.

We do. The little inn in the village of Puivert is also hosting sixteen Dutch tourists on a hiking holiday. Their English is good and their company boisterous. The castle of Puivert, with its beautiful block tower, is on all of our minds.

Speaking of the castles, one of the Dutchmen points out, "They all failed."

He's right. No matter how inhospitably situated, no matter how thick their walls or deep their moats, all the castles fell to the French crusaders from the north in the Cathar wars. Today the region proudly proclaims itself "Cathar country" and tour guides tell how the Cathars went into the bonfires singing. They are celebrated as martyrs and dissidents, possessed of the tragic romance of a lost cause. In a strange, backhanded way, locals also claim with pride that the French nation was born here: the twenty-year war against the Cathars was a crusade authorized by the Church and incentivized by the confiscation of Cathar lands. It was these two factors that allowed the French crown to extend its power over the Southern region. In this sense, the French nation was born on the ramparts of these failed castles, upon a blood sacrifice of Cathars.

One of the Dutch women asks if the Cathars influenced the Protestant reformation.

"They were wiped out," says someone.

"But did their ideas survive?"

Cathar theology—so far as anyone can reconstruct it—is tantalizingly Protestant in its critique of Catholic materialism, its use of women as prefects, and its determination to divide a "New Testament God" from an Old. All this was present in Cathar practice more than three hundred years before Martin Luther. Much of it, especially as regards the role of women, went far beyond him. But the beliefs are alien, too, from any Christian theology I know: to the Cathars, the God of Genesis *was* the Devil, and anyone who failed to achieve renunciation of the material world during this lifetime would be denied salvation and so remain trapped in a cycle of reincarnation.

None of us have an answer; the three centuries of unbroken Catholicism that follow the Cathar wars are a daunting obstacle.

We appeal to our host, who only shrugs and says, "Maybe," as she sets down a flan on the long table.

I remember first tasting flan in Ann Arbor, in the kitchen of a Puerto Rican friend. The dessert had come from Spain to Michigan by way of the Puerto Rican diaspora. Here in Puivert, the sweet custard reminds us that Spain is just fifty miles away and the border is an accident of bloody histories like the Cathars'.

I still wonder about the question. Is it only the lens of my own Presbyterianism that makes me feel Cathar-identified and makes me long for evidence of some survivance that goes beyond mere service as a regional mascot? I think of the Jewish Conversos in Spain, who survived the Inquisition by adopting at least a veneer of Catholicism. I first heard of the Conversos because some literary scholars theorize that Cervantes may have been one; it would explain the vein of religious tolerance that runs through his work. I try to bargain with the history of extermination here in Cathar country, wondering if there is any room in it for Cathar Conversos, for an unbroken chain, a contribution to the expanded possibilities of human imagination that somehow survived the fires of intolerance.

The Dutch guests will hike from Puivert for several days, but the host has been telling tales to them about our next stop at the village of Labau.

"Tell them!" they cry, prompting her to repeat the stories for our benefit.

"There is a village with only one man. He is very strange, I have heard," she says, raising her eyebrows and laying her finger alongside her lips in an exaggerated pantomime of curiosity. All the Dutch hikers look to us for reactions. It's only in the joking that I begin to wonder what it will be like to be two women traveling alone, riding up to stay with the last man in Labau. It seems unfair to tease us about the lonely circumstances that await us.

I know from our ride organizer that the village raised sheep until everyone moved away and that the last man went away, too, but has moved back home and is working to repair the village. Our part of the world, too, has ghost towns, lonely northern Michigan mining communities that have dwindled down to a single resident, gray wood weathering and drying up as if to blow away. I picture one of the little French crossroad villages we have been riding through, adding in more dilapidation, painting more cracks and an overgrowth of vines on the stucco and the orange roof tiles.

None of these pre-visions prepare us for Labau. For one, we don't come at it by road, let alone find it at a crossroads. We follow our directions over two fords at the foot of the mountain, pausing to let the horses drink. Then we find ourselves on a narrow trail that switchbacks as it climbs up a mountainside through deep, shady woods. We wonder increasingly if we're headed in the right direction. If we are not, this is my least favorite kind of accidental detour: one that spends our horses in climbing and winding and ends in fruitless backtracking. Our horses, trail-hardened and eager, knowing that dinner and pasture are nearby, surge up the slope. Finally, they burst out onto a sun-drenched, grassy terrace.

The last man in Labau is standing there. He's about fifty, wearing tiny cutoff denim shorts that show off a tanned body and rounded belly. But he isn't alone. He is surrounded by friends and family, the whole group enjoying wine and coffee under shade trees after a morning spent using a small concrete mixer to make repairs to his palatial and whimsically shaped spring-fed swimming pool. There's a laissez-faire attitude toward hosting us, so it takes a little while to find the tubs of horse feed, the suitcases, the room that will be ours.

After we hose off our horses and turn them out, we enjoy a plunge in the icy swimming pool and join the group under the trees. Another guest, a family friend, is slicing potatoes paper-thin for dinner. Soon someone takes out a jar of hash. After we decline to share the joint but assure them that we are not offended by it, a conversation on the state of marijuana legalization begins. I am surprised by how closely these people in this remote corner of France are tracking the legal landscape of the United States. In our home in Michigan, I offer, it is only legal as medicine.

The joint goes round, and all opinions, unsurprisingly, are strongly in favor of marijuana's harmlessness. "*La légalisation est aussi important parce que nous avons trop des prisonners,*" I say, offering as simply as I can my justice-oriented reasoning for supporting legalization. The last man's son launches into a quick, clear explanation of the crack-cocaine sentencing disparity. Our national shame is also well-tracked abroad. I'm again surprised at his knowledge of American jurisprudence and proud of my ability to follow the conversation, but then I hear him explain crack and cocaine as the drugs of the poor and the rich, respectively. I realize that I lack the vocabulary to insist that this is about race, not just class. It's another gap in my French education that may owe as much to France's post-colonial racial politics as America's. A moment ago, I was thrilled at being able to follow and offer ideas, but now I feel islanded by the lack of words.

As twilight gathers, the potatoes return to the table mixed up in a dish with duck meat, an exquisitely rich *confit de canard* that goes up and down the table until all are satisfied. Later still, someone brings out a cheese plate and sets it down in front of me and Mackenna. We both try to demur and let someone else slice first, but "You are our guests," they insist, suddenly standing on ceremony.

Mackenna takes the knife and makes herself three perfectly polite slices. I follow. I can hardly even get her to eat brie at home, but she surprises herself by enjoying not only the softest cheese but also its more pungent, aged counterparts.

After the cheese, there is music. The two young men pick their guitars with fast fingers, melodies that speak of the Spanish border just beyond the encircling mountains. Some songs are bluesy, too, reminding us how drawn-together this vast world is, how engaged in conversation.

Later, alone in our bedroom with the windows flung wide to the view of a mountainside that shows no further signs of human habitation in any direction, Mackenna and I laugh as she describes what was going through her head when the cheese course was set before her:

"I was so scared I was going to mess it up. I was like, I don't want to disrespect you, and your grandfathers, and your culture, and your cow!"

She saw the sacred in that plate of cheese, and I'm sure that she, far more conversant than I in the language of music, heard even more clearly the histories of global exchange that ran along the guitar frets. Not just to move through the world, but to understand it as we do so: isn't this what we seek every day of our lives?

It's strange that the wonder of it lets me sleep at all.

2019

July
Pony Girl

When my friend Halli texts to tell me that blood and flesh are protruding from under my mare's tail, I assume Ruby is having a uterine prolapse. This would not be unheard of in an old broodmare and is a condition that in horses tends to be a brief prelude to a fatal hemorrhage. I drive to the vet's office and pace out front, waiting for Halli to arrive with the trailer and trying to tell the universe that Ruby is too special to leave it in such a gruesome and senseless way.

Ruby presents a grim picture with her white tail and legs splashed with blood, but she seems not all that concerned, and even frisks my pockets for cookies as the vet examines her and announces that it's her bladder, not her uterus, attempting to slip out into the world. I hold her in the trailer in the parking lot as she has an epidural and a Caslick procedure to remodel her vaginal opening and help her internal organs stay internal. We're back home in just a few hours with steroids, antibiotics, wound care instructions, and a giant bottle of liquid equine birth-control.

Ruby takes it all in stride, but I'm well shaken. For days, I jump whenever I get a text message. I feel at peace only when I'm sitting in Halli's lawn on cool, dew-spangled mornings, watching Ruby graze after I've administered her medications.

Mortality is never far away when your horse is twenty-nine, but Ruby's near brush with it makes me contemplate the many crossings of stock, borders, and seas that it took to bring about this little mare. I begin poking around in her family tree. With time and patience, you can trace any Arabian's pedigree back to where it peters out and says simply "desert bred," marking the place where a horse—assuredly pedigreed in the oral history of its nomadic breeders—lost that piece of its heritage and passed into the hands of Egyptian or European owners who kept pedigrees in stud books. Within the Arabian breed, there are several pedigree families. I notice that, though her sire was the undistinguished product of someone's multi-generational efforts to breed Arabians with black coats, Ruby's dam was three-quarters Crabbet-bred, the product of a straight Crabbet sire and a half-Crabbet mare. Crabbet Arabians all descend from animals whom the Blunt family imported or bred in England at the Crabbet Stud, the origin point for European efforts to propagate purebred Arabians. The modern project of breeding "straight" or pure Crabbet Arabians like Ruby's grandsire always seemed to me a species of madness—a fetishization of the "eye" of the Blunt family to the point of serious inbreeding. I see a story glimmering in Ruby's pedigree, though. Generations of effort and intention had preceded my little mare with her five crosses to Raffles and her fifty-eight percent Crabbet blood, and strange chances had conspired to bring her into my hands.

Though Ruby is my first horse, my love of horses is lifelong. I can dimly remember a time when I saw every horse as beautiful, or when my eye was fooled by turnout—a flowing tail, neat mane, and glowing coat. Those who aspire to be serious horse people work hard to dispel this innocence in ourselves. We strive to gain an eye for the structure of a horse's body, to seek the legs straight and unblemished, the back short, heart girth deep, loin strong.

I grew up idolizing mentors who had the eye, who could go down to the New Holland horse auction and outbid the meat-buyers for a skinny, moth-eaten ex-racehorse who would blossom with good care into a show-ring star. As we develop our eye for horses, we learn to discard the shining or scuffed exterior and sometimes even the lack of good muscle, envisioning how a thin frame will fill out with the right feed and exercise. Where my little-girl vision might have simply led me to squeal "Horsie!" like kids do on a parade route, I've learned to say long back, cow hocks, straight shoulder, weak pasterns.

As a child I had riding lessons at a county stable, and at fourteen I became a volunteer at a therapeutic equestrian center. I branched out beyond my English training with a summer of guest-ranch work in Idaho and then hung up my stirrups for the most part, though I volunteered as a horse leader and sidewalker at another therapeutic equestrian center in Ann Arbor in my twenties and early thirties.

At most of these facilities, even when I was staff, I was insulated from the agricultural side of the horse business. Grain and hay arrived by truck. I remember once when I was in high school and the grain delivery was late, our barn ran out of senior feed. My boss instructed me to just feed the older horses regular pellets, but I quailed at making the sudden diet change. Instead, I drove to the feed store, thrilled with disobedience and generosity, and bought a fifty-pound sack of senior feed for sixteen dollars. I could hardly believe they sold it to me. Passing for a few minutes in wealthy suburban New Jersey as someone who might possibly own a horse felt more exhilarating than making an illegal alcohol purchase.

Even before I rode and worked with horses, I loved Thoroughbreds, beginning when I was old enough to sit on my father's shoulders to see over the rail of the saddling paddock at Monmouth Park. Later, some of the horses I grew up riding had been racehorses before they landed in the county stable. No wonder I long imagined that my someday-horse would be an ex-racehorse.

The Thoroughbred industry often speaks of horses in crops. Nearly twenty thousand horses were born in America's Thoroughbred foal class of 2018, hitting the ground from February to May. On January 1, 2019, they all became yearlings, a tidy piece of accounting imposed upon bodies at vastly different stages of maturation. One of these horses will win the Kentucky Derby in 2021, unless a foreign horse seizes that honor. One will win the Oaks. Five hundred will die young of illness or accident. Perhaps eighty lucky colts will join their fathers in the breeding barns, and two thousand fillies will someday retire to replace their mothers in the broodmare bands. A few thousand will find second careers. And—it wrings my heart far worse than the sudden and accidental breakdowns on the track—thirteen thousand will be reaped in slaughterhouses. Next year another nineteen or twenty thousand foals will start the same winnowing journey. Bringing home a racehorse of my own would be both an act of veneration for the breed's speed and elegance and my penance, an apology to all the horses I've cheered for over the years who were only taking a brief turn in the sun before a long one-way trailer ride to Canada or Mexico.

A few years after settling in the north, I felt as if I'd played out the local options for riding other people's horses and would have to make the leap to horse ownership just to get myself in the saddle. I found a boarding barn and filled out an adoption application with CANTER, a wonderful organization that places ex-racehorses.

And then I met Ruby. Or, rather, first I met Paula. She picked me out of the small crowd of spectators at a local horse show. She was a decade my senior, with long blonde hair and sharp, pretty features. She had the self-assured air of someone who was known and respected in the community, and soon I was firmly under her wing. I found myself shepherded to the snack bar and then given a volunteer task working the entry gate of the show ring. Then, before I knew it, she invited me to her place to go for a ride.

Paula's neighborhood in Lake Linden, a dense handful of homes carved out of farm country and woods, had a nearly suburban feeling. It seemed an unlikely place to find horses, but in a small, neat pole barn behind her house she kept three. I was there to meet the little gray Arabian, Ruby. Paula had owned Ruby for fifteen years, but the mare had spent the last few years earning her keep leased out to a succession of little girls before coming home for a break from packing kids. At twenty-eight, she was pushing the upward bounds of the equine lifespan, but she wore the age lightly and looked at me over the stall gate with her eyes bright and her sharp ears pricked.

Paula led the way on her big palomino quarter horse. Ruby walked alertly down the paved street in the neighborhood and then cheerfully trotted and cantered through woods and fields. As we surged up a steep and narrow trail and apple branches whipped my face, I laughed aloud. I felt myself coming to some understanding of the little mare I was riding. I fell in love with the way she said, "Yes, let's do this!" with her entire body the moment the trail got rough.

By July, Paula, Ruby, and I had all taken each other's measure and I had agreed to lease her. Then in September, Paula gave her to me. In one swift and stunning act of generosity, Paula engineered for herself a monthly board check and for her equine partner of fifteen years a safe and secure retirement right in her own barn. We sealed the arrangement with a hug in the barn aisle. I was a first-time horse owner at thirty-five.

A senior horse may seem a slightly dubious gift, sure to come with vet bills and heartbreak. But I do not believe that I am blinded by love when I say that in Ruby, I find no flaw. There are marks of age, the big ribcage of a little mare who's carried seven foals, and the extra fuzzy coat that comes with her Cushing's disease, a metabolic disorder that I manage with a small daily dose of pergolide. Many horses who have no business leaving descendants are bred each year, but I cannot say that they were wrong with Ruby. And much of what is pluperfect in her goes back to Crabbet.

As Ruby convalesces, I dive deeper down the Blunt family rabbit hole, summoning old and rare library books from all over the state. Lady Anne was the granddaughter of Lord Byron and a gifted athlete, equestrian, artist, and scholar of languages. In 1869 she married Wilfrid Blunt, whom their daughter later described as "an amazingly handsome and splendid but utterly lawless young firebrand whose brilliant and hypnotic personality enslaved half the women in Europe, and was destined to be her first joy and her last tragedy." Judith's description of her father contains both condemnation and admiration, as if she sees through his passionate, Romantic facade to the philandering and callow man beneath but somehow still celebrates his charm. I study Wilfrid, who gazes intensely out of an albumen portrait. He strikes me as a cut-rate Byron. Like his wife's grandfather, Wilfrid was a traveler, revolutionary, poet, and womanizer who carved a wide swath of destruction in his personal relations.

Anne and Wilfrid's shared passion for adventurous travel and fine horses was the best of their partnership. For years, they spent each summer in Egypt or present-day Saudi Arabia, making long horse-buying expeditions on camel and horseback. Lord Byron shared and prefigured the Blunts' fascination with the Islamic world. In 1813, the same year he published *The Giaour,* the first of his Oriental Romances, Byron posed for a portrait in Albanian dress, resplendent in a red and gold jacket and a loosely wrapped turban. The painting helps confirm a connection between Byron and the eponymous main character of the poem. The Giaour is, like most of Byron's main characters, so nearly a self-insertion that the entire trope of the passionate and volatile Romantic hero is known in the English tradition as a Byronic hero, adjectivizing him in a way that blurs author and character. The word *giaour* is a Turkish pejorative term for a non-Muslim. As the Giaour enters into combat with his nemesis Hassan, Hassan declares, "I know him by his jet-black barb; / though now arrayed in Arnaut garb." Arnaut is a word for Albanian—so the Giaour astride his black horse is, like Byron, a Westerner in Albanian dress.

For both the Giaour and Byron, this clothing choice symbolizes their global wandering and stands for a rejection of the confines of English social expectations. Wilfrid Blunt followed in Byron's footsteps and appeared in numerous portraits in "Arab dress," favoring flowing Bedouin-style robes and an agal and headscarf instead of a turban. In one oil painting, he is princely, facing the viewer with a hawk on his arm, a curved knife on his hip, and a greyhound at heel. In another, painted by Anne, he easily sits a rearing horse, a rifle clasped in one hand, apparently unconcerned to be teetering on the edge of a rocky outcropping, much as the Giaour "spurs his steed; he nears the steep, / that, jutting, shadows o'er the deep."

Byron's poem begins with the dramatic image of the Giaour galloping along the Athenian cliffs, too late to save his beloved Leila. At first glance, this failed effort to rescue her from a life in the harem and from her husband Hassan's murdering hand seems to replicate a common colonial trope: that of the supposedly-enlightened Western man wishing to save Middle Eastern women from Middle Eastern men. The poem reveals, however, that the Giaour knows that Hassan "did but what I [the Giaour] had done / Had she been false to more than one,"—that is, he, too, would have murdered Leila if she were unfaithful to him. Men, Eastern or Western, present no good options for Leila, who never appears in the poem alive. Even the fisherman who rows Hassan into the "channeled waters dark and deep" so that Hassan can drown her only sees in the murderer's arms a swathed "burthen" that "doubtless [holds] some precious freight." To the Giaour she was "a form of Life and Light," and what she may have been to herself or wanted for her life neither the Giaour nor the poem trouble to inquire.

Wilfrid was no more prepared than Byron to compass a woman of Lady Anne's mettle. On their Arabian journeys the Blunts crossed the Tigris and Euphrates and survived sandstorms and bandits. During these long desert treks, Anne comes off the more impressive figure of the pair: she spoke fluent Arabic; she rode for days with a dislocated knee; in camp she doctored horses or mended saddles while "Wilfrid slept in the shade of his tent unconscious of any obligation to lend a hand."

The horsewomen I run with share my deep suspicion of horsepeople like Wilfrid who get the reins and glory handed to them by others who do the hard, daily work of horse care. The Blunts had money on a scale that we untitled mortals can hardly imagine and might have fixed on any silly thing to spend it on. They chose horses. They could travel, and ride, and they had the eye—and, oh, could they buy horses. Anne and Wilfrid and, later, Judith bought and transported and bred fine Arabian horses on a scale that forever shaped the genetics and geographic distribution of the Arabian breed and, so, the modern horse world. Yet at some level, I believe that Wilfrid did not know horses.

Since becoming a horse owner in the north country, I have come to know the calculus of horses and land on a more intimate level. Horse hay is a local matter here, a commodity that's too bulky to ship for long distances and is better hurried across town on summer afternoons when no rain clouds threaten.

That first summer I knew Ruby, Paula's friend Farmer Rodney mowed a borrowed field up on Gay Road; he ran his rickety old baler over the dried piles of grass, yielding square bales that I caught, balancing on the swaying trailer as they came up the conveyor. Paula took the bales from me and heaved them high to stack them tight and neat. I cursed this baler every time we had to toss hay that season. It always left one of the two binding strings just a little too loose, and the bales were liable to come apart on impact.

The tractor and baler were of a similar vintage. Before we left the farmyard, I watched Rodney take an egg from one of his hens, lift the steaming radiator cap, and crack it into the radiator to seal a leak and coax the tractor into doing just one more job.

We squirreled the hay away anywhere we could. We packed it all the way to the super-heated rafters of Paula's pole barn, sweltering in thick dust and heat as we clambered fifteen feet up the pile of hay to tuck the top bales in. It didn't all fit there, so we also used the hayloft of Rodney's old cow barn, one of those gray, weathered farm structures that seems to cling to life through storm and wind and snow because it would take too much effort to fall down. We parked round bales in a shed on his place, too, a generosity that made the entire system work, since keeping hay dry takes at least as much effort and planning as making it in the first place.

A thousand-pound round bale can keep Ruby and two of her horse friends for a week. Paula fed round bales as long as she could—until the mud or snow got too thick to get the pickup truck into the pasture to drop them off, and then she switched to the more expensive, laborious square bales that we delivered to the field on foot, hefting one in each hand.

Farmer Rodney can pull five round bales off an acre, so it's no exaggeration to say that almost four acres of grass in this town are standing just for my little mare. Sometimes I like to ride Ruby past Rodney's field, a high, lifting place from which you can just see Lake Superior shining in the distance. We go by in spring when the road shoulders first open and the field sleeps long and lazy into April under its late blanket of snow. In May and June, we watch the grass grow, bright and sweet, past her knees, reaching for her chest. You're the queen of this field, I tell her. It's here for you.

Whether we dress it up in tall boots or dress it down in redneck pride, horse ownership has at its core this astonishing privilege: the ability to tell four or five acres exactly what to do. A cowboy hat is good shelter from the sun, as well as being a piece of Americana. It's a settler-colonial identity symbol inspired by U.S. Cavalry uniforms—wearing it is wearing the appropriation of land, the extermination of buffalo, the massacre of indigenous peoples. I prefer a helmet. We who jump fences or have kids to come home to or earn a living by our minds like a little extra skull protection, and the Stetson always feels to me like cowboy drag, no matter how many trail hours I log in a Western saddle and cowboy boots. I grew up in the other American horse culture—the style derived from the foxhunter's uniform, in the tradition of the English aristocrat's assertion that he may follow the hounds wheresoever he pleases, with no *Sorry!* or *By your leave, peasants!* for passing through your fields. The horse is a formidable symbol of war and class assertion, associations that cannot be escaped, whatever the costume.

For all Wilfrid's revolutionary politics, the Blunts' grand desert adventures are part and parcel of pre-World War I European imperialism. Wilfrid criticized Egypt's colonial status but enjoyed a rich colonist's lifestyle nonetheless. He purchased an apricot orchard outside Cairo to create the

Blunts' Sheykh Obeyd Stud Farm and stocked it with some of the finest Arabian horses in Egypt, buying them from wealthy Egyptian breeders who had fallen on hard times. In 1878, the Blunts, still hungry for more horses, pursued their quest into the Arabian horses' homeland. They rode through the Najd Desert in present-day Saudi Arabia, attended by servants and local agents, buying the best horses they could lay their hands on in order to "preserve" the bloodstock which they feared was in danger due to growing pressures on nomadic lifestyles as the region modernized. The Bedouins they encountered were often reluctant to sell their most prized horses, especially to Europeans, but the Blunts had wealth, persistence, and a willingness to sometimes hide their identity as purchasers behind local intermediaries.

In March of that year, midway through the journey, Wilfrid rode Ariel, "the loveliest of all the mares" they had bought, on a wild boar hunt. The mare stood unflinching before the charge as Wilfrid shot a large boar, but her courage was her undoing. She was gored, and an artery in her hind leg was severed. Wilfrid and his companions were able to staunch the bleeding and then made the unthinkable decision to lead her on for ten miles, including a deep river crossing. When she collapsed on the second day, the Blunts left her in the care of an Arab servant with instructions to meet them in Baghdad with her if she survived. They never saw her again. This mare, who "had a perfection of type and beauty seldom seen" and whom Anne eulogized as "the noblest and best and gentlest creature," was thus lost in the course of Wilfrid's afternoon entertainment.

In the same decade, the German archaeologist Heinrich Schliemann also engaged in "preservation." He conducted hasty excavations on the site of ancient Troy that smashed straight through his goal, the Odyssean layer of the city, and destroyed much of what remained of it. Despite the violence of the excavations, he found a treasure in gold and silver artifacts that he named Priam's Treasure, including two diadems he referred to as the "Jewels of Helen" though they came from a layer several centuries deeper than Helen's day. Schliemann's wife, Sophia, posed for a portrait wearing the jewels, and Schliemann boasted that Sophia had smuggled the treasure away from the dig site by wrapping it in her shawl. Sophia's involvement was exaggerated, but the smuggling was real: the artifacts were illegally removed from the Ottoman Empire and ultimately wound up in Berlin. They disappeared during the Battle of Berlin at the end of World War II; it was not until 1994 that Russia admitted to capturing the artifacts and housing them in Moscow, where they remain today. The collecting activities of both the Blunts and the Schliemanns dislocated treasures from their lands of origin under the justification of "preservation" when they did not destroy them entirely in the grasping.

Much of the Blunts' popular appeal lies in their status as some of the most traveled Europeans in the Middle East of the Victorian era. One contemporary British commentator trumpeted Anne's journey across the arid Najd plateau to the city of Ha'il in 1881 as the first such journey "ever undertaken by a woman," a proclamation that treats the region's thousands of female residents as if they don't exist or don't count. To this day, Arabian horse exhibitors in the United States deck themselves and their horses in brocade and tassels for a "Native Costume Class" contested in a blinged-out version of nineteenth-century Bedouin dress. It seems less about playing Arab than about playing Lady Anne playing Arab, as if they, too, had ridden the far deserts of the East to come back with these exotic horses.

At home in England after they founded the Crabbet Stud in 1878, Anne and Wilfrid swam against the tide of England's affection for tall Thoroughbreds when importing, breeding, and marketing the pony-sized Arabians. The Blunts' horses were not the first Arabians to reach England. In fact, the eighteenth century had brought to England the foundation stallions—Arabians, Barbs, and Turkish horses—that created the English Thoroughbred when crossed upon the local mares. And even those local horses had been refined for centuries by ones brought back from the Crusades. The strong, fleet horses of the East have always been tempting as prizes of war and military assets. It gives me a wry smile to think about how, if I've loved Thoroughbreds all my life, I've loved them for the spirit and eager athleticism that they inherited from these desert-bred ancestors in both waves of importation. To love an Arabian is to go back to the source. But here were the Blunts with these treasures wrested from the East and hardly anyone they could convince to admire them.

England was the backdrop on which Wilfrid Blunt's worst qualities played out. The Blunts' marriage and family life came under pressure from Wilfrid's many affairs, his wild spending habits, and his prolonged fury at his inability to completely separate Lady Anne from her money due to the peculiarities of her title and inheritance. The Crabbet Stud was a passion for them both, but it was also a vehicle for financial abuse, as Anne's money purchased the horses and Wilfrid then sold them off and pocketed the cash for his other habits. Wilfrid's often impulsive and sometimes spiteful sales helped drive the dispersal of Crabbet Arabians across the globe—to the United States, Japan, Australia, South Africa, Indonesia, and Poland.

Matters between Wilfrid and Anne reached a head in 1906 when Wilfrid moved one of his mistresses into their home, proclaiming a desire to live in what he considered to be the Eastern polygamous style. Anne separated from him, taking herself permanently to the Sheykh Obeyd farm in Egypt and successfully maneuvering to protect part of the Crabbet Stud from Wilfrid by leaving it in the hands of their daughter, Judith, a skilled horsewoman in her own right. After Anne's death in 1917, Anne's horses passed to Judith and her children. Wilfrid mounted legal challenges to the will and even resorted to nighttime horse-napping and horse murder.

In some ways, there is nothing remarkable about this story at all. Animals have always found themselves tossed on the winds of human fortunes. Many an abusive spouse in an unravelling domestic situation has threatened or harmed the animals of a family as a means of controlling or hurting the people in it. It is completely ordinary in its monstrousness. Perhaps I find it haunting because Wilfrid's urge toward ordinary monstrousness trumped the thesis of his life's work with Arabian horses, the idea that these little, then-unfashionable horses from the desert should be prized above all others. The same Wilfrid who wrote flippantly toward the end of World War I that the stud was "a more important issue perhaps than that of the British Empire for which Haig is fighting, in as much as the horse is more worthy than the man," was the man who shot the prized mare Bukra because she was too heavily pregnant to travel on the night he came to steal her from his own daughter.

I have Wilfrid's biography shipped north from Flint just to see how his biographer will handle the horse shooting. Elizabeth Longford has nothing on the death of Bukra, and only glancing reference to the death of one of the seven other horses whom Wilfrid destroyed out of spite. She writes: "On Armistice Day Judith put ribbons in her own and her ponies' hair, but heard that Newbuildings had celebrated by shooting Regiz, lest she should get him." Judith, however childishly depicted here, was forty-five years old, and, of course, the buildings across Crabbet Park did not shoot the horse; Wilfrid or his order did.

Earlier this summer, Paula was preparing to exit a suffocating marriage. She had perhaps at some half-conscious level been preparing for it even when she met me and set in motion the reduction of her responsibilities from two horses to one. With Paula giving up her place, I had the chance to take Ruby where I chose—and to appreciate just how charmed it had been to be right there with Paula. The woods and fields around her home had become our landscape. There is a culvert on the snowmobile trail east of her place that is safe on the left and perilous on the right, the pipe rusted straight through. Once a porcupine sat in a birch tree and watched us make the crossing. There is an old dead poplar tree that marks the place where we turned to avoid another unsafe culvert. As we took our last rides there, I was aware that it was another landscape tattooed on my heart that I wouldn't travel any longer.

My first year with Ruby took us on mile after mile of trails; to horse shows where we competed in halter, English cross rails, and Western pleasure; to parades; and even, once, swimming in Lake Superior. There were days when the snowshoe hares were piebald, half-dressed for winter, and they showed themselves leaping away through the underbrush, and when a coyote watched us from just off the trail. Deeper in autumn, these days yielded to others when the snow was a soft, thin blanket, not yet locking us in, and we cantered through the winter woods, each branch picked out by its tracing of snow, and I could scarcely believe this was a life I get to live. Along the way, I found friendships with Paula and Halli and other women in their circle that resonated with an understanding that started at the barn but circled out into our lives as daughters, partners, parents, and dreamers. I felt lucky in every way as we prepared to move Ruby from Paula's house to Halli's.

I'd heard enough horror stories of animals who became assets or casualties in contested divorces, so Paula and I registered Ruby's bill of sale with the Arabian Horse Association and made my ownership of her real on paper just before Ruby's twenty-ninth birthday. We moved all the useful farm equipment and even the stalls from Paula's barn to Halli's. I helped Paula pack books, haul furniture, and remove the weapons from her home for her final weeks there. She reassured me that she was safe, but her act of forethought made me worry. I held my breath and fervently hoped that happiness was waiting for her down the road.

Paula found herself a beautiful little bachelor's cottage and moved there without crisis. Ruby's transition was less smooth. Her bladder prolapse came about just a few days after arriving at Halli's house, when her old broodmare's body responded to the dubious allure of the single gelding on the property by entering such an enthusiastic heat cycle that she turned her own body inside-out and sent us all scrambling for the vet's office to seek treatment for the world's most unexpected side-effect of divorce. As with so much else, my friends and I got through it together.

When the ownership of the Crabbet horses and Lady Anne Blunt's estate was finally litigated in 1919, Wilfrid pled ill health and insisted that the high court come to him. He received the judge and lawyers in his brocaded bedchamber, dressed in "scarlet and silk Arabian robes reclining on a carved Spanish bed with Oriental hangings." He was perhaps aiming for majestic, but at age seventy-nine and glassy with morphine, the effect was merely eccentric and pathetic. The project of trying to wring from his daughter and grandchildren the last remnant of the fortune he had failed to steal from his wife during her lifetime was ghastly. In this, Wilfrid seemed to live out a curse laid on Byron's Giaour.

After Hassan's death, someone—the speaker is unclear but perhaps it is Hassan's mother (in a passage widely credited with spawning English-language vampire literature)—curses the Giaour to become a vampire "unquenched, unquenchable." The curse runs:

> Thy corse shall from its tomb be rent:
> Then ghastly haunt thy native place,
> And suck the blood of all thy race;
> There from thy daughter, sister, wife,
> At midnight drain the stream of life;
> Yet loathe the banquet which perforce
> Must feed thy livid living corse:
> Thy victims ere they yet expire
> Shall know the demon for their sire.

Wilfrid had lived, finally, to become that vampire, having stolen his wife's happiness and now clawing at the rest of his family. The courts sided with Judith and the Crabbet Stud lived on, safe under her management until her death in 1957, rather than being consumed in Wilfrid's gambling and romantic debts. In 1925, Judith bred her great Polish import Skowronek to his daughter, Rifala, to produce Raffles; this little gray horse was imported to America in 1932 and bred to his own daughter Rafla to produce Rapture, one of his best sons and Ruby's great-great-grandsire.

At just 13.3 hands, Raffles was a full two inches shorter than Ruby, also pure white, and famous for his beautiful, classically-shaped Arabian head; his endurance and athleticism; his high, proud action; and his ability to sire foals who looked just like him. Though Raffles was born in 1926, the line-breeding to him on the Crabbet side of Ruby's pedigree is so persistent that it simulates time-travel. Raffles accounts for one-sixteenth of her total genetic makeup, on par with ancestors born in the 1960s. To explain her short stature, the proud set of her neck, the flag of her tail, and her willingness to go down the trail for mile upon mile, one need look no farther.

Like Ruby, Raffles was a tough old horse. He was twenty-three when he suffered a terrible leg break and spent sixteen weeks recovering in a plaster cast and a full-body sling, but he went on to live to the age of twenty-seven and sire another fifteen foals to carry on his legacy and help stamp American Arabians forever in his image. I'm back in the saddle riding gently before Ruby's stitches are even out, and we're running through the woods again by autumn.

Once I had dinner with the writer Percival Everett at a conference, and the talk, already Western, turned to mules and horses. I shared that I was just a few weeks into horse ownership and bashfully admitted that my horse—my pony, really—was a 14.1 hand Arabian, perhaps an odd choice of mount for a six-foot tall woman. Everett, with the wit and generosity that characterized our entire interaction, just said, "Now, an Arabian is like a sports car. You might have to stick your elbow out the window. But the performance!"

I think of his summation often when I'm with my mare, especially in those moments when the ground is right and, even though we're already cantering, I throw the reins up her neck and kiss to her just to feel the leaping joy of her acceleration into a winging gallop.

Arabians were bred for millennia to survive, travel long distances, and make war in desert environments, but for the past hundred years or so, under the Blunts and those who followed them, it has been mostly for this: to thrill their riders with their willing speed, beauty, and spirit.

Horses are both biology and material culture. Just like art, architecture, and fashion, their bodies are modified by selective breeding to suit changing tastes. Today, Egyptian Arabians descending from the ones imported to Egypt by Abbas Pasha (much as Crabbet Arabians descend from ones owned by the Blunts) are also bred all over the world and have a distinct look, as if they are Arabians exaggerated. Their eyes are bigger, their noses smaller, faces more dished, throatlatches more delicate, and their necks more long and graceful. They flirt with caricature the same way that Arabian costume classes Disneyfy Bedouin clothing.

But sometimes horses, unlike other forms of dislocated cultural patrimony that languish in museums or mutate in the cultural imagination, can thrive and adapt in new environments. One hundred and forty years after the Blunts brought Arabian horses to England, a Michigan Tech student from Saudi Arabia approached Ruby and me as we prepared to carry the flags of the host colleges at the Parade of Nations and asked me, "Is she a pony?"

"She's an Arabian," I answered, as the student stroked her nose.

Then she beamed up at me and said, "I thought so. She should walk with me!"

Now in Ruby's thirtieth year, we are both drinking deeply of our best life. We give riding lessons to a young family friend who experienced a paralyzing illness, and it's a joy to be close to her in her first months of recovery, to watch her progress from using a wheelchair to crutches to a cane. In spring, she takes Ruby on the trails, covering five to ten miles with me at the leadrope and her father sidewalking. There's an intimacy with the horse that I feel when I'm on the lead rope, different but not less than the connection of being in the saddle. I walk beside Ruby, keeping my touch light so as to not interfere as she listens to her rider and navigates the terrain. It feels so easy and natural to enjoy the outdoors with these friends that I sometimes wonder why more people don't go hiking this way.

In the heat of this first Covid summer, we take solo jaunts and long rides with friends. We take dressage lessons. We give my grandbaby pony rides and take a friend's seven-year-old to a local speed show and finish first or second in every class in the leadline division, each ribbon feeling like a public proclamation that I have the best horse in the county. The joy I find in sharing Ruby with her many friends teaches me something of how Paula could bear to give her away to me.

I doubt that Lady Anne Blunt, wrapped in her final desert retreat, could have pictured a Crabbet descendent living this treasured, ordinary life in a remote northern place, but I like to think she might have looked with approval on Ruby's small, sturdy frame and her ability to live long and do and be all these things. She is, after all, one of the many branching endpoints of the Crabbet legacy.

August
The Electric Girl

I pick up Naomi Alderman's *The Power* the week after our national martial arts tournament, and rarely has a book presented itself to me as such a cathartic projection of my own life. Like electric eels, Alderman's women can shock people who touch them. In one of the opening chapters, before the world has truly understood the women's newly emerged power, a girl named Roxy is cornered by a home invader.

> He reaches for her with one hand, the knife in the other. She gets ready to kick him or punch him but some instinct tells her a new thing. She grabs his wrist. She *twists* something quite deep inside her chest, as if she'd always known how to do it. He tries to wriggle out of her grip, but it's too late.... There's a crackling flash and a sound like a paper snapper.

The man falls back, stunned. For Roxy it is instinct heeded, power wielded. She doesn't know what she's done, quite. I know the feeling. I have been that electric girl.

The first time I was groped, I might have been twelve. I don't remember the year, but I remember the pain as my undeveloped breast was squeezed, and I remember the swift arc that my backfist carved in the air. That single, windmilling assertion broke the assailant's grip and his nose.

But that was only the first time. It is not always convenient, safe, or adaptive to break someone's nose. There's blood, and attention, and sometimes even a little guilt.

Not much guilt, though. The electric girl is in one sense lucky because her body, not she, makes the decision to do harm. She can blame the aggressor, not her own knuckles. I thank martial arts for that. But on days when her reflexes are not wound so tight, or the assault is not so sudden, and she has a moment to weigh the costs, sometimes a victim chooses sufferance.

It is easy to valorize the electric girl and to think that she might change the world. My elder daughter, Heliena, is also a black belt. One Fourth of July, flooding away from the docks in an after-fireworks crowd, someone walking behind us touched her, and she turned with a loud "Hey! Don't touch me!" and the fierce look that said she would be ready to back it up. The young man jumped three paces backward. I have another friend who has been known to Judo toss men in the street when they put their hands on her body or her hair. An American hero. God bless the electric girls for their refusal to merely flinch and hurry on.

The martial arts community to which I belong often expresses a collective belief that if more women and girls defended our persons with violence, there might be less violence directed at us. Alderman's book explores this premise. As the women become aware of their power, and men become aware of the women's power, cultures change. Women decide who and when to shock; soon women rule, and women hurt, and women torture and rape. It was only those first-awakening girls who shocked others unaware, not knowing what it was they did. The book's strongest chapters are these early ones, as the victims find themselves suddenly able to turn the tables on attackers and abusers. Meanwhile, the men involved confront an upending of what they thought they knew about women. In one such scene, two teens, Tunde and Enuma, tussle over a can of Coke by a swimming pool. I appreciate the subtleness of the way this scene begins. The teens are both laughing, but then Tunde puts his body weight on Enuma.

> She's laughing, and he's laughing. He leans his body weight into her; she's warm underneath him.
>
> "Do you think you can keep it from me?" He lunges again, and she twists to escape him.
>
> He makes a grab at her waist.
>
> She puts her hand to his.... There is a feeling as if some insect has stung him.... He cannot move his left arm.... She is still giggling, soft and low. She leans forward and pulls him closer to her.... He is afraid. He is excited. He realizes that he could not stop her, whatever she wanted to do now.

When Tunde puts his weight on Enuma, the play of forcefulness sets off some jolt of fear in her—a situation, perhaps, that many of us can relate to, when a moment seems to totter and tip from safe to dangerous. Here Enuma's instinctual "No" manifests instantly as an electrical impulse, not only within her nervous system, but externally, shocking Tunde. "He is excited" may be the only wrong note in Alderman's description. Tunde is in the position of the woman who finds herself, yes, perhaps desiring, but also suddenly knowing that she lacks the physical ability to enforce a "No," should she utter it, and who finds herself weighing the safety and desirability of raising her voice in such a situation. Is it better to silently half-acquiesce than to risk it all on a No being honored, with the physical and psychic violence of a rape being the consequence of a No ignored? Who has the capacity to assess one's own desires while performing such a risk calculus?

Tunde was once the architect of this encounter, the one who arranged for them to be alone, the one who teased her about the Coke and closed the gap between them. The insight dancing here is that Tunde's ability to shape the scene depended upon his physical strength and safety. Now that Enuma is stronger, he is transformed into a passive participant. Now she sets the terms. She kisses him, then runs away and dives into the pool. He never gets to say No or Yes.

This scene invites us to ponder: what if women could, like Enuma, say No with an expectation of safety? How would this revise men's notions of what is consensual and what is pressured? Tunde did not seem to understand how his size, weight, and strength were impacting their flirtation until Enuma's electric shock reversed their roles.

As the novel advances, I do not care for Alderman's idea that power begets cruelty in an inevitable progression. Women having the ability to back up a No need not lead to female street gangs, crime syndicates, and rape squads. In my life as a martial arts instructor, I devote myself to the idea that more strength and power can lead to confidence, peace, and safety, even if I also cannot quite believe the wishful thinking that there is a critical mass of women's self-defense ability at which male violence against women would cease.

There is a story about my childhood instructor, Master Morey, that I often tell my students to set the stage for their first lessons in self-defense. Master Morey is now an eighth dan, the highest-ranking female master in the art of Soo Bahk Do. She's almost as famous for her temper as for her fighting ability, a volatile, hard-edged woman who came to the top of the art when there were not many other women around her to share the road. I began training with her when I was only six years old. She had a stern leadership style that never left room for me to wonder if women belonged in martial arts, a grace in motion that stole your breath, and a reverse punch you didn't want to stand in front of.

Here's the story: Master Morey was once walking in New York when a man stepped out of an alley and grabbed her by the wrist. This is, absurdly, the exact first scenario I will train my students for, though it's rather rare in truth: a bad guy grabs your wrist, right hand to right hand. My students learn it by rote from their first weeks as white belts: escape the grip; gain control of your attacker; strike to neutralize them; leave the situation. What did Master Morey do, with decades of training and hundreds of techniques to choose from?

I always pause here, playing up the moment and the formidableness of the woman, enjoying the dramatic irony. Everyone who hears this story knows exactly who this foolish man has just put his hands on.

Master Morey looked the man in the eyes and said, "You don't want to do this."

He saw something in her eyes that he didn't want to tangle with. He simply said, "Oh!" as he let go of her wrist and walked away.

I promise to train my students in a few techniques for escaping an assault in progress, ways to improve a situation that has already gone deeply awry. But I want them to learn these techniques knowing that a longer commitment to the martial way might eventually lead them to this other place, this transcendent confidence that allowed Master Morey to do no harm when she might have harmed this man most grievously.

There are many things I love about this story and the way I use it. It's a chance to impart the lesson that peace is the strongest and most admirable choice. It lets me give others a glimpse of the power embodied in a woman who meant everything to my childhood and whose legacy I continue in my dojang every day. I want this legacy of strength and confidence for myself and my students, especially the female ones.

I have reservations, however. I don't know how to read the assailant's "Oh" in that long-ago New York. If he simply slunk back into his alley and waited for a less formidable victim to walk past, then there was not much victory here.

The age of YouTube gives us all opportunities to savor the surveillance footage and cell phone videos that capture the moments when petite female black belts give attackers the surprise of their lives. But what does that surprise teach? The revelation the world needs is not a man's surprise that a woman is formidable and will be hard to harm; it's the universal realization that she is human. Until such a realization settles into our culture, all of the self-defense training I can provide runs the risk of just passing the experience of victimhood down to the next, less-prepared victim, and of encouraging a victim-blaming complacency where we look at the world and shake our heads, murmuring, "Women should learn to defend themselves."

Self-defense skills will never be enough. I have walked this world for twenty years and more with the power to do great harm contained in my body just like Alderman's electric girls. It's as much a part of me as the specialized skein of muscle and nerve that nestles under the collarbones of the women in *The Power*. My strength, my arm's length, the precise maximum height, speed, and reach of each of my kicks are part of how I measure the world and position myself in it. It is at least as formidable as an inborn taser.

But sometimes, on the subway car, it is not clear to whom a groping hand belongs. Sometimes, embarrassment or fear stops us from raising a shout. Women are socialized to be quiet and to be embarrassed by sexual situations, including unwanted ones. Sometimes that embarrassment gets us assaulted or raped or lets our rapists walk free afterward.

One of my friends said something to me about all this that was a balm to my soul. She said that she honored the frozen me, the woman who was choosing other survival strategies or defaulting to them out of shock or fear.

For six and a half years, I had once- or twice-yearly encounters with a man in my martial art. It began with inappropriate comments at a tournament. It was my homecoming competition, a shaky and new-fledged return to the art after eleven years away. I was twenty-nine; I hadn't been in regular training since before I finished high school. But, alone in a new town, trying to write a dissertation and not lose my mind for lack of chances to get out of the house, I'd wandered into a dojang of another martial art and started kicking again. My return was going well; I'd won the women's sparring division and was preparing to spar the male winners in the championship bracket. This man approached me and the college student I was about to spar.

"It's kind of like a date," he said. Then he looked at the young man and said, "Try not to screw it up." His rank was his shield. Whether he knew it or not, and I suspect at some level he did, his rank was what kept us from scoffing outright. We were, in any case, unable to leave the side of the ring to which we'd been called for competition, so we squirmed while we attempted to politely deflect the stream of comments.

It was a relief when our match was called. We entered the ring and for two minutes, the world outside its four corners blurred. The adrenaline of a sparring match sometimes leaves me with little memory of the fight, but I remember snatches: the serious intensity with which we squared off; pushing myself to fight inside, an inversion of my usual strategy since I was, in this rare case, the shorter person in the ring; the terrible, bright popping sensation in my hamstring as I reached a hook kick past my opponent's face. I scored the point and ground my molars into my mouthguard as we squared off again. The hamstring sang with pain when I tried to lift my right leg. I was now down one kicking leg and doing my best to show nothing of it on my face. I lost a close match and felt no regrets—I was too full of the happy thrill of having competed at this level, of having found an opponent so worthy, and of being home at last, back in the ring after eleven years away.

Afterward, the young man took me aside and apologized for the older man's comments. I appreciated his kindness and grace, but I told him that he did not need to distance himself from this man: the way he had treated me in the ring during our sparring match told me everything I needed to know about the seriousness and respect with which he treated female peers. I took so much heart in the way this young man offered me his witness. This other man had behaved embarrassingly; it felt, perhaps, like enough to speak together of how we'd endured him. I shared my experience with the tournament organizer in the weeks after the event but passed up his offer to address the comments. I didn't want to make a fuss. I feared how raising a complaint would color future meetings with this embarrassing elder. Mostly, though, I looked forward to sharing the ring again with the kind young man and the other new friends I had made that day.

My return to the art was paved by generous and trustworthy men. Master Steyer in Boston saw me at the tournament and told me of Master Scholz, in medical residency on my side of Massachusetts. I met up with him at a gym in North Adams and later in his yard. In two- and three-hour workouts, he poured knowledge and time into me, fine-tuning my long-rusted techniques. I was inclined to look backward and regret how long I'd been away, to apologize as our lessons covered green-belt and red-belt material as well as black-belt requirements. He combatted this by setting my eyes not just on my next test but on the one after that: for my fourth dan. Several times each workout, he would begin sentences with, "When you go to Ko Dan Ja." Not if. When. All my life I had heard of Ko Dan Ja, the eight-day-long test that draws our practitioners together from around the continent and makes masters out of third dans, but never before had I heard someone tell me that I was going.

When Master Scholz finished his residency and went to a posting at Walter Reed, I attended my first national tournament since my homecoming and there met Master Cortese, another master without a studio. Seventy years old, imposing but cheerful, he had been one of the first generation of Americans to come home from Osan Air Force Base with a black belt, had been part of founding the Soo Bahk Do organization in the United States. Master Steyer was a student of a student of one of his students. Master Cortese was retired from both teaching high school and studio owning, but when he learned that I lived less than thirty miles from him, he took me on. I went to meet him in his home, where we went to the basement, made room by stacking the coffee table on top of the sofa, and began the preparations for my third dan test in earnest. I went back twice a week for more than two years.

If the circumstances of these meetings ever goosed me—Meeting Master Scholz for the first time in a gym in a town I didn't frequent or taking private lessons from Master Cortese in a basement—the men themselves quickly put me at ease. They allowed me to shed shyness and apology and to take my place in the line again.

Over the years, though, there were other encounters with the elder from the tournament. I acquired a radar for his presence as soon as I entered event spaces. I began positioning myself in rooms so as to keep him out of my line of sight, hoping that by pretending he was invisible and slighting him as much as I felt able, I could avoid future conversations. But he had a knack for finding me when I was standing in line, anchored in place by protocol. He made excuses to touch me. A female instructor I'd known most of my life peeled him off when he flung himself on me to hug me in New Jersey because he liked my forearm bruises. "Look into trigger point therapy," he said to me at the next tournament in California, providing unsolicited medical advice while poking me under the clavicle with a gun made from his fingers. "This way you'll remember."

"Trigger." *(poke)*

"Point." *(poke)*

"Therapy." (*poke*)

I have not forgotten wanting to break his fingers.

Oregon. Six years after my return. In a little more than a year's time, I hope to test for my own Master Instructor certification and fourth dan rank. Getting there will require an even more intense training regimen than I already enjoy, eight days off for the test during the school year that I will need to move heaven and earth to acquire, and no small amount of money. In some ways, I have been preparing for this test for almost thirty years.

I am proud of Soo Bahk Do's tradition for these testings. It gives our art a consistent technical standardization the world over. It gives our ranks greater meaning. The group of people from around the nation with whom I test in 2021 will hopefully test with me for fifth dan in 2026 and sixth dan in 2032. The eight-day physical and mental ordeal of Ko Dan Ja forges testing classes into tight networks of friends who tell stories of each other, meet up with joy at tournaments, and pass around itinerant students like me. I have not yet been to Ko Dan Ja, but I have already benefited from what it does for our art. But if I must spend eight days in monastic confinement with my harasser, scanning every room for his presence, it will not be the eight days for which I have worked these thirty years.

This point is driven home to me when Ko Dan Ja candidates are asked to identify ourselves at the national tournament in Oregon so that a high-ranking instructor can take us downstairs to a small conference room and put us through our paces. The man, who has no business in this group, tails me down the corridor, puts his hand on my shoulder, and speaks into my ear his intention to sit in on our clinic and take notes.

I shake him off my shoulder without responding. I continue down the hall, scurrying to put more people between myself and him. I feel myself bristling all over with unspent electrical impulses. I wish I was still that twelve-year-old girl who backfisted faster than thought or that I could have made the decision to impersonate her. In this moment, I do not value my own peace quite enough to hurt someone for it.

One of the themes the instructor of our clinic is driving home for us is the need to move together as we execute our forms and basic motions. Though the two dozen candidates in the room are from far-flung areas of the country and many of us have never met before, we are all expected to breathe together, begin our motions together, finish together. To do so requires an almost extrasensory attention with ears and peripheral vision to one's classmates. I try to achieve all this while those very same senses are also tuned to the presence of the man in the back of the room who for six years has shadowed my experiences in the art.

This is not the experience I want for my Ko Dan Ja test. I have to move to protect it. I've been thinking and writing on Alexie and Me Too, thinking on the way the paths of women are strewn with harm in so many areas of our lives, and that gives me the strength to do it. After the clinic wraps up, I ask the leader if I can speak with him and the man.

When I have the three of us in a rough triangle, I address my harasser. "On the way downstairs, you put your hand on my shoulder and spoke into my ear. I didn't like that. I'm exhausted by the level of effort I put in at national events to keep your hands off me. I need you to never touch me again." The instructor whom I've gambled to recruit as my witness simply says, "And that's all that needs to be said."

This would be a fine place for the story to end: confrontation and affirming support. It would be a nicer ending had not that man gone straight upstairs to bend Master Cortese's ear, an intrusion into my relationship with my own instructor that feels like yet another violation. I do not want to converse about this with Master Cortese, a man whom

I respect and love like a second father. Master Cortese wonders why I did not come to him for help. Come to him *quietly* for help is the unspoken word I hear. The truth is that I love him too much to have had the courage to risk it. Had I approached him and received the wrong, unsupportive answer, that relationship might never have been the same. I'd made the choice not to put him to the test. For this reason, I resented my harasser's tale-carrying all the more.

Mad world that it is, I am ashamed for having been harassed. I am so invested in being my instructor's star pupil that I am afraid that this harasser's behavior has rendered me less-than, or more-trouble-than, a male student. Now with my back to the wall, at this crisis point I did not ask for, I insist, bravely and out loud, that I am not open to being criticized for my handling of the incident. My instructor hears me, and he responds more gently. Silently, though, I continue to do quite enough of that criticism myself.

While my harasser likely never felt the need to reflect upon his actions until I made them into a source of public embarrassment, I have invested many hours in imagining the things I might have done or said, and I will never know what might have been the effect of speaking up—or striking out—sooner. I will only know in time how the effects of my moment of confrontation, and this act of telling of it, may ripple out from here.

It is far more life-giving and heartening to reflect upon the things that came together for me to make my confrontation: allies, witnesses, a sense of annoyance at years of effort spent in deflection and avoidance, systemic reflection on how women the world over and in all areas of life engage in such efforts, and, finally, a confidence that I belong in the space that no doubt traces to the fierce female instructor who first welcomed me into it. I have had power enough for years, but I would still like to learn how to speak with her confidence to anyone who tries to use my gender to treat me as insufficient or as a novelty or an ornament or a victim: "You don't want to do this."

2020

August
The End of Something

This pandemic will be the end. I've been braced for the university's failure for four years, ever since the first autumn my family was with me, when the university slashed our health and retirement benefits. The moment drove home the precariousness of the institution in ways that my modest salary and the campus's often cracked and peeling infrastructure had not. That moment was my introduction to a new type of pain, a wounding of a barely-grown piece of my identity as breadwinner. I had felt so much pride and pleasure in providing my family with a home, a stable income, health and dental insurance, and a plan for further education. Now I walked a whole new avenue of fear about the future I was leading them into.

Long-time employees told me stories of encountering other long-ago employees, retirees who gave them the dubious reassurance that our university had never had glory days, had always somehow teetered on the brink but never closed. This was meant as reassurance, and perhaps also as an expression of the make-do Yooper pride so prevalent in this town.

We faculty spend the Covid summer living in two realities: in one, we battle with administrators in meetings and memos, afire with the passionate attempt to preserve course offerings, faculty lines, academic freedom, and a livable wage for our junior colleagues. We struggle for the soul of the university to remain true to some kind of educational mission as if we expect there will be a university in the fall. In the other reality, we know that if the virus is spiking, if the students stay home, if the fall sports are cancelled, if the safe opening plan sounds too perilous or insufficiently fun, the fragile equation of tuition revenue and expenses will shatter. I don't think there will even be enough cash in reserve for a teach-out to graduate our seniors and give our other students time to make graceful transfer plans. We could shutter up and blow away overnight.

My family lives in both disaster and futurity, too. Mackenna is preparing to enter trade school (if school will convene), and my husband and I are preparing our home in hopes of welcoming two or three more children. We attend trainings, meet with our social worker, and paint and furnish bedrooms despite being braced for sudden and simultaneous job losses that we fear may sabotage our application to foster and adopt.

As I contemplate the prospect of another national job search, I know that my chances of success in a more-than-decimated market are slim. And I know that I don't want to leave this place. For these children I haven't met yet, and for the chance to raise them here, I will take what work I'm lucky enough to find. I became a professor because I wanted to use my life in service to a teaching vocation and a social-justice mission. It's a determination that has gotten battered along the way but has never left me. For five years, it was my life. Now I'm grateful to these future children for giving me an off-ramp, a chance to try on my husband's frank, blue-collar mindset and let work mean food on the table and cash in the hand for the many other pieces of life that matter.

August brings a gathering-in of summer, even as our thoughts begin to turn to fall. We eye our wood pile and make our last wood-gathering runs. I used to have a wood guy, a young man named Heidegger who often came with his toddler son as co-pilot, who brought me cut and split wood by the pickup truckload. Then the summer of the Father's Day flood brought down so many trees in our town that wood was piled all over, a waste and an annoyance. My husband and I took our wood delivery money, bought a chainsaw, and committed ourselves to a lifestyle of wood scavenging. That first year, we cut logs until we could lift them awkwardly into his Jeep or a borrowed pickup, then brought them home for further cutting and hand splitting with an axe or maul.

This year, my husband spent the summer creating a twenty-foot-long home-built trailer equipped with a winch, a seven-foot-tall steel arch on the tailgate, and a pair of wickedly sharp vintage logging tongs. Shortly after the trailer is finished and plated, he sees a roadside sign for free wood. The power company has taken down some massive trees near the powerlines, and the land-owner wishes they were gone. Shawn arranges to come back that afternoon.

The land-owners, a pair of elderly Finns with beers in hand, heckle and advise as Shawn backs the trailer into position near the embankment. I get out and take a look at what's here. The power company stripped the limbs off and left the logs in fifteen- and twenty-foot sections. There's what looks to have been a spruce tree or two, plus an ash that must have been a true monster, three feet in diameter at the base. When the trailer is ready, I walk the winch line up the bank, spread the logging tongs at their widest, and set them on the bark. I love this tool for its simple ingeniousness; when the winch puts tension on the line, the tongs will pull closed and bite even more firmly into the bark. I jump well clear before the log starts sliding and rolling down the bank.

One good bite will get the log through the ditch and up to the tailgate. I leave the joystick-like winch controller to Shawn and stay on hand to move the winch line and the chain to the steel arch, which we can then use to raise the log and swing it aboard the trailer. The Finns produce a long crowbar and are surprisingly helpful at prying and persuading the massive logs to make a neat load in the trailer. We finally turn for home, babying the Jeep along well under the speed limit with the massive load behind it.

We have friends up here who heat entirely with wood who are always nodding at our newness to making firewood by repeating to us the proverb that firewood warms you three times: when you cut it, when you split it, and finally when you burn it. And it is sweaty work, leaving us sticky with sap, grimed with sawdust, and ready to fall into bed and sleep deep and hard at the end of the day, then wake up to cutting and splitting.

These satisfying physical tasks have their opposing twin in my teaching preparations. I go to my office, pull a thumb tack from the stack of papers on my cork board, the first of which just says, "Next Time," and review my yearlong jotted list of regrets and proposed changes and excited ideas for future iterations of my courses. My mind begins to race along on three different syllabuses all at once as I wrestle with myself over the assignment sequences and final text selections. This year there's the additional question of delivery modes, online first and last weeks, and backup delivery modes to prepare for the event of students in quarantine or the region in lockdown. It's an explosion of parameters. Still, just like any other August, I begin to pester my university's long-suffering librarians with interlibrary loan requests for supporting texts. Used books begin to overflow from my mailbox. Writing seems to take a greater act of will each day, a determined push to hold the semester at bay just a few hours more.

Attending to the garden helps quiet the roil of my mind. I carry buckets of rain water, cut dahlias, harvest tomatoes, basil, beans, and peas. I watch hopefully as winter squash and watermelon grow without attention from mice and chipmunks. It's also time for picking wild thimbleberries and preserving their sweetness in jams and freezers.

The last week before my fall teaching contract begins, we clear two days on our calendar and I let my husband bounce me in his jeep to a favorite spot where pebble beaches extend into Lake Superior over gray extrusions of bedrock. The soilless shore sparkles clear to a great depth. As we walk up the beach, our steps rattle in the gray and purple pebbles like a sack of coins tossed on a table. This is the treasure. We scramble along the outcroppings and small islands, the terrain and the splash of waves making us unabashedly playful. I choose the brightest, bluest place and give my body to the cold water.

Dragonflies spar in squadrons over our campsite, and at night the stars rotate overhead. After the moon sets, Saturn is so bright in the eastern sky that it leaves a trail of light in the smooth, black waters of the lake like a road that leads to the first kindling wisps of dawn.

In the morning, on our trail out, I pick and eat berries until my fingers and lips are stained bright red. Later, at home, sipping the syrup from the bottom of the berry pail, I think that if the Upper Peninsula had wood fairies, this bright, wild, sour-sweet juice would be their drink. It's fit for a fairy queen. Ends-of-seasons always seem sweet to me, and this year, if possible, the end of summer is even sweeter than before. A season of life is also folding itself inexorably away. We'll be here, waiting beside Lake Superior, for whatever the next season brings.

Acknowledgments

The essays in this volume rest on the work of other writers who have accompanied me in my life and my teaching, whether as friends, mentors, references, or bugbears. "August: Migration" leans on Tiya Miles' brilliant history *Dawn of Detroit.* "October: Pomegranates" relies on Andrea Scarpino's "Madonna of the Pomegranate" and "Self Portrait as Pomegranate" from her book *Once, Then.* "October: Apples and Time Machines" deals with Kurt Vonnegut's *Slaughterhouse-Five,* Octavia Butler's *Kindred,* Audrey Niffenegger's *The Time Traveler's Wife,* and the film of the same name. "November: How We Make Do" uses Virginia Woolf's *A Room of One's Own,* while "December: Grandbaby" uses Barbara Kingsolver's *Prodigal Summer.*

"January: Raccoons and Salmon" describes teaching Mary Oliver's "The Fish" and "Raccoons" from *Twelve Moons.* "February: Gun of Innocence" uses Vievee Francis' "Gun of Wishes" from *Horse in the Dark: Poems.*

"February: From Mea Culpa to Me Too," the essay on Sherman Alexie, draws from "Amusements," "Jesus Christ's Half Brother is Alive and Well on the Spokane Indian Reservation," "The Approximate Size of My Favorite Tumor," and other stories in *The Lone Ranger and Tonto Fistfight in Heaven,* as well as on *The Absolutely True Diary of a Part-Time Indian,* on his February 28, 2018 press release, and on a 2012 interview with Belinda Luscombe for *Time.* The essay's more admiring engagements include Denis Johnson's "Car Crash While Hitchhiking" from *Jesus' Son*; Nalo Hopkinson's *Brown Girl in the Ring*; Louise Erdrich's

LaRose; Stephen Graham Jones' *Mongrels*; Roxanne Dunbar-Ortiz's *An Indigenous Peoples' History of the United States*; Margaret Noodin's *Weweni*; Rebecca Roanhorse's *Trail of Lightning*; Tiffany Midge's *Bury My Heart at Chuck E. Cheese's*; and Beth Piatote's play, *Antíkoni,* from *The Beadworkers.*

"March: Copper Dogs and Gold" relies upon Gary Paulsen's *Winterdance.* "April: Attic Rooms" uses Margaret Atwood's *Handmaid's Tale* and her March 2017 essay in the *New York Times Book Review*, as well as Harriet Jacobs' *Incidents in the Life of a Slave Girl,* Frederick Douglass' *Narrative of the Life of Frederick Douglass, An American Slave*, and Ibram X. Kendi's *Stamped from the Beginning.* "June: Little Stranger" uses Rebecca Solnit's writing on Virginia Woolf in the titular essay from *The Mother of All Questions*, and also touches on her books *Hope in the Dark* and *Savage Dreams.*

The French essays, "July: La Belle-Mere" and "July: Labau," draw upon Dan Savage's *The Kid* and David Lebovitz's *Sweet Life in Paris,* with passing references to Marjorie Margolies' *They Came to Stay*, Percival Everett's *Half an Inch of Water*, Lisa Hilton's *Athénaïs*, David Downie's *Paris, Paris*, and the Charles River Editors' *The Cathars.* For "July: Pony Girl," Lady Wentworth (Judith Blunt)'s *The Authentic Arabian Horse and His Descendants* was useful for Judith Blunt's reflections, numerous art plates, and excerpts of Anne Blunt's diaries and other contemporary writings, including a piece by Theodore Cook. Elizabeth Longford's biography *Pilgrimage of Passion: The Life of Wilfrid Scawen Blunt* and Lucy McDiarmid's *The Poets and the Peacock Dinner* were useful in considering Wilfrid Blunt's legacy, as was, in its own way, Lord Byron's *The Giaour*. Finally, "August: The Electric Girl" takes off from Naomi Alderman's *The Power.*

Before these essays came to press, Lynette Yorgey and Angela Watrous were my readers when I needed them most. "January: Raccoons and Salmon" first appeared as "February: Raccoons and Salmon" in *Identity Theory* in March 2018. "October: Pomegranates" was published in *Up North Literary Journal*, Summer 2018. "From Mea Culpa to Me Too" first appeared in *Waccamaw* 23 in Fall 2019. "Copper Dogs and Gold," was performed for the Red Jacket Jamboree variety radio show, 14 February 2020. I'm grateful to the editors, including Colin Burch at *Waccamaw*, Jesse Rice-Evans at *Identity Theory*, Jacob Lindberg at *Up North*, Rebecca Glotfelty of Real People Media, and Diane Goettel at Black Lawrence Press for understanding and believing in this project.

Above all, I'm grateful to the family members, students, and friends who have shared this season of life with me and trusted me to include their stories in this book.

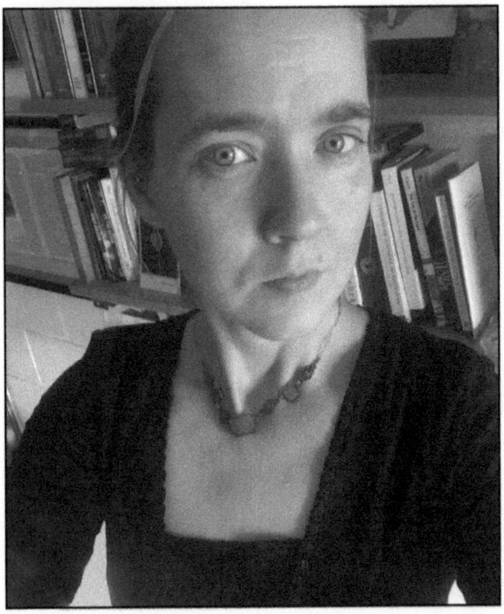

Carolyn J. Dekker holds a BA in Biology and English from Williams College and a PhD in literature from the University of Michigan. She lives in Michigan's Upper Peninsula and teaches English at Finlandia University. Her creative nonfiction has appeared in *Identity Theory*, *Up North Literary Journal*, and *Waccamaw*. She has published scholarship on Jean Toomer, Leslie Marmon Silko, Willa Cather, and Emily St. John Mandel, and edited Jean Toomer's *A Drama of the Southwest* for the University of New Mexico Press.